M

THE BASICS

The global economy is dominated by a powerful set of established and emerging capitalisms, from the long-standing capitalist economies of the West to the rising economies of the BRIC (Brazil, Russia, India and China) countries. An understanding of capitalism is therefore fundamental to understanding the modern world. *Capitalism: The Basics* is an accessible introduction to a variety of capitalisms and explores key topics such as:

- the history of major capitalist economies;
- the central role played by both states and markets in the global economy;
- the impact of capitalism on wages, workers and welfare;
- approaches to the analysis of capitalism, and choices for capitalism's future.

Examining capitalism from both above and below, featuring a range of case studies from around the globe, and including a comprehensive glossary, this book is the ideal introduction for students studying capitalism.

David Coates holds the Worrell Chair in Anglo-American Studies at Wake Forest University in North Carolina, USA.

The Basics

The reach of capitalism is increasing, impacting on more and more people. As recent events have shown, capitalism is a dynamic system prone to crises. David Coates has produced a concise, yet comprehensive account of capitalism, providing key insights into its origins, dynamism, consequences, and possible trajectory. It is an invaluable resource for all students of capitalism.

Matthew Allen, *Senior Lecturer in Organisation Studies Manchester Business School, University of Manchester, UK*

David Coates, one of the pre-eminent scholars of capitalism, has produced in this introductory volume another compelling contribution to the debate. It will make an excellent starting point for new waves of scholars interrogating the nature of capitalism. The book is very coherently and cogently structured to achieve very effective coverage of all the key issues, topics and debates. More importantly it is written in a lively style bringing to bear a vast array of historical and comparative insights and examples to inform a lucid, reflective critical account of capitalism's past, present and future.

Ben Clift, *Professor of Political Economy, Department of Politics and International Studies, University of Warwick, UK*

Anyone looking to understand the basic tenets of capitalism, both from above and from below, should read this superb book. David Coates has written perhaps the best introduction to capitalism there is out there, and he has done so with panache and erudition. By tackling the history, the variety, and the consequences of capitalism in a truly balanced manner and with scholarly sophistication, Coates encourages his reader to chart capitalism's future. A whole new generation of students will greatly benefit and learn from Coates' insights and humanity.

Matthias Matthijs, *Assistant Professor of International Political Economy, Johns Hopkins University, SAIS, USA*

CAPITALISM
THE BASICS

David Coates

Routledge
Taylor & Francis Group
LONDON AND NEW YORK

First published 2016
by Routledge
2 Park Square, Milton Park, Abingdon, Oxon OX14 4RN

and by Routledge
711 Third Avenue, New York, NY 10017

Routledge is an imprint of the Taylor & Francis Group, an informa business

British Library Cataloguing in Publication Data
A catalogue record for this book is available from the British Library

Library of Congress Cataloging in Publication Data
  Coates, David, 1946-
  Capitalism : the basics / David Coates.
  pages cm. -- (The basics)
  Includes bibliographical references.
  1. Capitalism. I. Title.
  HB501.C627 2016
  330.12'2--dc23
  2015011545

ISBN: 978-0-415-87091-7 (hbk)
ISBN: 978-0-415-87092-4 (pbk)
ISBN: 978-0-203-79879-9 (ebk)

Typeset in Bembo and Scala Sans
by Florence Production Ltd, Stoodleigh, Devon, UK

Printed and bound in the United States of America by Edwards Brothers Malloy
on sustainably sourced paper

For Eileen,

as she starts another stage in our great shared adventure

CONTENTS

ILLUSTRATIONS

FIGURES

TABLES

PREFACE

Capitalism has been with us for a long time now, and so has already attracted to itself a vast literature of commentary and critique. Anyone writing a new volume on capitalism, of the kind awaiting you here, owes you therefore at least a preliminary justification for adding yet another book to the many already available. My justification is broadly two-fold.

Much of the existing literature on capitalism is decidedly partisan. Some of it is enthusiastically advocatory. That is particularly true of a recent literature written by mainly American scholars that is openly supportive of a capitalism only lightly regulated by public policy. Some of the more established literature on capitalism, by contrast, was and remains highly critical of it—advocating either the tight management or the entire replacement of capitalist ways of organizing an economy. At the very least, therefore, someone coming new to the topic may well benefit from a balanced guide to this on-going conversation about capitalism and its consequences. Providing that guide is one reason for everything that follows.

But there is more. Capitalism is not only a controversial way of organizing the production of the goods and services that are now so central to modern life. It is also a highly dynamic and ever-changing way of organizing that production. So dynamic and ever changing, in fact, that any specification of its central characteristics and consequences requires at the very least a regular and extensive updating of data sets and coverage. That updating is especially needed now, since the global capitalist system as a whole has recently been fundamentally transformed. It has been fundamentally transformed partly by the collapse of the Soviet Union and the entry of communist China into capitalist world production on a vast scale; and it has also been fundamentally transformed by the severity of the global financial crisis and subsequent recession that began in the United States in 2008. What follows, therefore, is both a guide to the history and present trajectory of contemporary capitalism, and an overview of the debate on the determinants of that trajectory.

I

Two general but necessary elements of what follows need to be recognized before we begin. The first is that because capitalism has been around for such a long time (and because over that long history the performance of capitalist economies has varied between capitalisms and changed from one time period to another) any understanding of the performance of capitalism in the contemporary period requires first a full understanding of capitalism's performance in the past. To know where we are now requires that we explore exactly where we have been, and determine from whence we have come. So there is a lot of *history* to be told in the pages that follow—history about capitalism as an economic system and history about the people who delivered it.

Moreover, because those changes in the ways in which capitalist economies operate have been both substantial and controversial, the generations which have experienced them have regularly discussed and debated their desirability. So in addition to bringing historical data to bear on the question of contemporary capitalism and its future—in addition, that is, to discussing capitalism in the medium of *time*—we will also need to discuss it through the lenses of the competing theoretical systems that have struggled to understand and to change the way in which capitalist economies work. So there will be a serious engagement, in the pages that follow, with bodies of *theory* as well as with bodies of history. Indeed, it is the putting of the two bodies together that should help clarify the basic character of capitalism, and so meet the main purpose of a book published in a series dedicated to the exploration of basic concepts.

And in relation to both theory and history—as is only appropriate given the way capitalism uses markets to allocate resources—there will also be regular opportunities for you to choose between the theories on offer and the histories being told. As we will see, *choice* and capitalism necessarily go together in the way capitalist economies operate, so it is only right and proper that choice and capitalism should go together in any serious commentary on that practice. For that reason, you will find yourself, as you read on, being periodically given the opportunity to make at least a preliminary judgment on the adequacy and desirability of the capitalist world opening up in the pages before you.

II

The longevity of capitalism and its dynamism have one other major consequence for us as we begin. They make it essential that we develop and use as precise and as consistent a set of terms and meanings as we can manage. Complex things such as capitalism, if they are to be grasped accurately in all their totality, require the deployment of an equally complex lexicon. (Williams, 1976; Braudel, 1982: 232–48; Hodgson, 2014) So for our purposes here, we will conceive of capitalism as a way of organizing an economy, and when we speak of "capitalism" we will mean simply the economy. We will use the term as a *noun* for that purpose. But since, as a way of organizing an economy, capitalism has had (and continues to have) such an impact on the way we all live, and has that impact regardless of whether we are directly involved in the economy or not, we will also use the related term "capitalist" as an *adjective*. We will talk, for example, of "capitalist societies" and mean by that term whole social formations organized around (and profoundly influenced) by an economy that is run on capitalist lines.

As a noun, we will also often use the term "capitalism" as something limited by an adjective! In fact, you can expect to meet a lot of hyphenated nouns in the pages that follow—and to do so for three important reasons. First, because capitalism develops over time, it will sometimes be necessary to differentiate "early capitalism" from "late capitalism," or "fully developed capitalisms" from "developing" ones. Then, because capitalism does not develop in all places at the same time but rather stretches out from some places to others, it will sometimes be necessary to differentiate "core capitalisms" from "peripheral" ones, and to differentiate developed capitalisms in the "North" of the globe from less developed capitalisms in the "South." And finally, because, even when fully established, capitalist economies vary in the ways in which both governments and social orders are organized around them, it will sometimes be necessary to differentiate "liberal capitalisms" from "coordinated" ones, and "welfare capitalisms" from capitalisms with less developed welfare states; and throughout, "free market" capitalism from more "managed"/ "regulated" forms. Yet for all this necessary differentiation, each of the economies so labeled will be a "capitalist" one, which means that our first task has to be that of establishing what it is that they all have in common that makes them "capitalist." Only then will we go on to trace the rich variety of capitalist forms that now populate an increasingly integrated global economic world.

III

In putting this introduction together, I have had great help from Colin Tyler, Michaelle Browers and Eileen Coates; from the two external readers at Routledge; and over the longer period from the wonderful students with whom I have regularly shared a first-year seminar on "Debating Capitalism." I am grateful to them all. I just hope that their insights show through in the chapters that follow. I promise I have tried!

David Coates,
Wake Forest University
March 2015

WHAT IS CAPITALISM?

The vast majority of people reading this book will have bought it—the vast majority but not everyone. That the vast majority will have bought it tells us something about the ubiquity of buying and selling in modern life. That others of you may have received it as a gift, or borrowed it for a brief period from a public library, reminds us that there are dimensions of our modern condition that are not so commercialized. And that yet others (I hope not too many) may have "liberated" it from the bookshop without paying for it reminds us that, even when buying and selling is the normal order of the day, not everyone respects the rules of private property on which most modern commercial activities ultimately depend.

Welcome to the world of capitalism. It is a world in which most things are bought and sold, some things are lent or given away, and yet others are stolen and held illegally. It is a world of things that people make and sell, things the vast majority of which are both privately owned and privately consumed.

THE UBIQUITY OF MODERN CAPITALISM

The most immediately striking feature of the modern capitalist condition is its ubiquity. If you are some modern British version of a Christopher Columbus, as I once was, keen to leave old Europe to find your way to untold riches in the West, then if your decision was to fly from London to New York on Continental Airlines, their plane will bring you directly to Newark Airport in New Jersey. Landing there will provide you with your first glance of the New World. What will that first view be? Not the one Christopher Columbus had—of that you can be certain. He first saw Arawak people fishing, hunting and cultivating land for their own immediate use in an economy that "shared property, land, food, canoes and tools." (Logie, 2013). You, by contrast, will likely first see New Jersey Americans who will definitely not be fishing or hunting, and certainly not sharing property and land. The first New Jersey Americans you are likely to see will actually be shopping—shopping at the huge IKEA store that is situated just the other side of the New Jersey Turnpike. The store is enormous—so enormous, in fact, that depending on which side of the plane you happen to be sitting, you simply can't miss it as you land. It's one of the biggest things around, replete with the obligatory blue-covered exterior walls and large yellow lettering—a retail outlet which both in appearance and content will be virtually identical to the IKEA store in which you could have shopped at Brent Cross in London immediately before you set out on your transatlantic adventure. Unlike Christopher Columbus, that is, you may have left Europe behind but parts of Europe will have definitely gone before you.

Not that you need travel so far to recognize just how all-pervasive is modern consumer capitalism. You can discover that merely by traveling down several high/main streets in the particular part of North America, Western Europe or Australasia in which you happen to live (if that is your condition), or by spending several nights watching any travel program on the global television networks that now penetrate the modern private home. In the English-speaking world at least, high streets can look remarkably similar these days: a standard mixture of (often similarly named) retail stores, fast-food restaurants, car showrooms and banking institutions. Not that every high street is the same—that is still one of the charms of traveling, discovering the local and the anachronistic—but each high street now has a far higher chance of similarity to others far away than it had even thirty years ago. And on those streets—in those retail stores, restaurants and banks—money now changes hands at a quicker pace and in greater volume than hitherto, as the number, quality and range of **commodities**[1] available for sale expands exponentially from one generation to the next. Those of us who live in capitalist economies probably have parents and grandparents who also lived in them, but who did not live in them in the material comfort that most of us now enjoy.

It is not just <u>consumption</u> that is increasingly similar in so many parts of the world these days. The way <u>production is organized</u> is increasingly similar too. In country after country, people leave their homes on a daily basis to go to work in factories and offices that are organized in much the same way no matter where they are. The number of days those people go to work each week, the number of hours they spend at work each day, the pay they receive for each hour worked, and the intensity of the work they do in return for that payment—all these things vary both between countries and over time in any one of them. But normally these days there is never enough time in any working day in any modern economy for most people to combine all their work and domestic responsibilities without having themselves to rush. In the towns and cities of the modern world, people rush back and forth between where they live and where they work, giving themselves unprecedented levels of personal stress as they do so and placing on the urban areas through which they move unprecedented demands on transport systems, on local public resources (schools, hospitals and the like), and even on the quality of local natural resources (not least water and air).

Post-2008, many of the towns and cities in what we will later recognize as core capitalist economies probably also share levels of job insecurity and involuntary unemployment greater than in their own immediate past—particularly unemployment among adults at both the start and the end of their working-age decades. They will certainly be surrounded by rural and suburban areas with recognizably common characteristics that have also changed over time. They will be surrounded by rural areas that are now increasingly depopulated, with lower standards of consumption for those left behind than for those who have departed for town. They will be more immediately surrounded by ever expanding

[handwritten margin note: working + housework = productivity]

suburban areas in which more and more people currently choose to raise their families and spend their leisure time, but from which many of them now increasingly depart on a daily basis to go elsewhere to earn the money to do so.

We live these days, that is, in an increasingly globalized capitalist world, many parts of which are beginning to look remarkably similar. But even today, not every part of the global system looks the same. Vast swathes of whole subcontinents (the Indian, the North Asian and the African) remain locked in forms of production, and levels of consumption, still relatively untouched by the global spread of capitalist forms of production and consumption. For our purposes, however, it is the character and spread of those capitalist forms on which we will need to concentrate. We will need to do so both because they *are* spreading, and because their character is *impacting* economic and social life in every corner of the global order in ways in which the remaining pockets of non-capitalist activity most decidedly are not.

Capitalism is really the only show in town these days, and so we do need slowly and steadily to establish exactly what sort of show it happens to be. As a starting premise, let us for now understand capitalism as an economic system in which the vast majority of goods and services produced are produced to be sold— and sold at a profit. People do not go to work in capitalist economies, as they have in many differently organized kinds of economy in the past, in order to produce things that they themselves immediately consume. They go to work in capitalist economies in order to make things that are then sold to others. They also go to work because that is the only way in which they can earn the money that they need in order to buy things they require but now no longer make themselves—to buy things, that is, that are made by other people. In an economy run on capitalist lines people sell their own labor power, the better to buy things made by the labor of others. Or to put it more technically: *capitalism, when fully developed, is best understood as a system of generalized commodity production driven by the pursuit of profit and based on free wage labor* (based on labor, that is, that is provided in exchange for a money wage).

[handwritten margin note: make things to sell to people in order to buy things made by others]

THE EMERGENCE OF MODERN CAPITALISM

To fully grasp both the character and modernity of this thing called capitalism, it is important to recognize from the outset that the major economies of the world were not always organized on capitalist lines. In fact, in the full span of human time, capitalism is an extremely new phenomenon, one that is still even now only in the process of full formation. Economies in the far past invariably developed a sector in which goods were bought and sold. At least they did so as soon as at least some of their people settled in towns and stopped working exclusively on the land. There were, that is, sectors within them that foreshadowed the capitalism to come. And it is certainly the case that in some, although only some, of the pre-modern civilizations with which our history is replete—particularly that of classical Rome—coinage was plentiful, trade networks were eventually extensive, and scales of manufacture were historically unprecedented. Indeed the Roman Empire at its peak in the first and second centuries AD maintained urban populations of a scale not seen again in Europe until the seventeenth century, and did so on the basis of agrarian and manufacturing production in which slave labor played the dominant part, and particularly via the movement of grain products over considerable distances. Rome was fed in the last centuries of the Western Empire in no small measure by grain grown in Egypt. For as Rome defeated its enemies it enslaved their populations and forced many of them into large-scale agricultural production, and it was from those large-scale farms that Roman landowners then sold grain either directly to the Roman state or to the privileged consuming classes of the empire's urban centers. (Coates, 2015a: 53–80)

But in the western end of the Roman Empire at least, slave-based commodity production ultimately gave way to what we now recognize as European feudalism, a far less productive system of predominantly agrarian production in which a peasantry tied in different ways to the land produced just enough food and raw materials to sustain themselves at a subsistence level and to sustain those who controlled them (mainly a landed aristocracy and its supporting clergy) at a slightly higher standard of life. For at least five centuries after the fall of Rome in 476 AD, levels of urbanization in what had once been the Western Empire remained modest—well below peak Roman standards—and trade in goods became localized where it survived at all. (Wickham, 2005: 699) Only slowly, and mainly from the eleventh century, did feudal Europe begin to develop large-scale urban centers again—Italy once more leading the way. Only slowly did Western European trade pick up in volume and range (McCormick, 2001: 778–798): trade between town and country, and trade between an under-developed Christian Europe and a more economically advanced Muslim empire then dominant in the southern Mediterranean and the Near East. And so only slowly did a class of men (and it was almost exclusively men) emerge whose economic survival depended on the production and sale of the goods so traded. Only slowly, that is, and initially only in certain regions, did European feudalism witness the emergence of a limited level of commercial capitalist economic activity. It was from those modest beginnings that eventually modern capitalism was to grow. (Braudel, 1984)

There is a considerable debate in the relevant academic literatures about why all this occurred. There is a debate—sadly beyond our concerns here—about why Rome fell, and about the necessary limits of slave-based production as a form of long-term economic activity. There is another debate—much more germane for us—about why feudalism eventually was replaced. (Hilton, 1976) There is also a debate about why Western Europe should have emerged as the cradle of a new form of economic activity that would eventually become globally dominant. (Mielants, 2007) The debate on "the transition from feudalism to capitalism" ultimately turns on whether the key causal drivers in play—the forces eroding feudalism—were forces anchored within feudalism itself, or forces released by the interplay between an under-developed European feudalism and the more economically and intellectually developed Arab world to its South and East. There are two key *internal* drivers in play in this debate. One was the role played by feudal Europe's uniquely independent network of city-states in the consolidation of commercial capitalism. The other was the changing balance of class forces in the feudal countryside, the ultimately inadequate supply of peasant labor that obliged landowners slowly to monetarize the relationship between landlord and serf: the demographic impact of the Black Death being particularly significant here. The key *external* driver, often cited by way of contrast, was the growing trade in luxury goods between Western Europe and the Levant that characterized the late medieval period, with ruling groups in feudal Europe slowly commercializing their agricultural holdings in order to generate commodities with which to trade. The three drivers may well all have operated in concert. The Black Death arrived, after all, on the backs of plague-infected rats (or possibly gerbils) brought to Messina in Sicily, and to Genoa and Venice in Italy, by trading ships returning from the Black Sea. But either way, by the fifteenth century at least, the flow of goods within and beyond Europe was beginning to quicken—not least through ports such as Venice—and with it the spread of capitalist ways of organizing economic life: first through northern Italy and then up the Rhine and on into the rest of Northern Europe. (Braudel, 1984)

The "transition from feudalism" debate and that on "the rise of the West" both recognize that, throughout what we now term the late medieval period, feudal Europe's main economic characteristic was its *under-development*—under-development relative to the Europe that would follow, and under-development relative to the economies and societies immediately beyond its borders: those in the Arab world and, further away still, those in both India and China. Paradoxical as it may well have seemed when first underway, capitalism developed fastest where societies were least sophisticated; and in its development helped to eventually invert entirely the power relationships of the pre-modern global order. But the paradox was actually more apparent than real, because new economic systems always pose a threat to the distribution of social prestige and political power predicated on the existing economic order, and so emerge more readily where those existing systems are too weak to control them. In the powerful monarchies of the pre-modern Middle East, commercial activity remained firmly subordinate to aristocratic political control. It was in the weak monarchies and fragmented political units of pre-modern Europe that towns could win their independence from local rural control, and powerful burgher classes could emerge who were both willing and able to develop commercial (and eventually even primitive industrial) production. Independent cities were strongest in Western Europe after 1400 initially in both Italy and northern Germany, and it was in them—and in the trade between them—that what became Western capitalism was first cradled into life. (Arrighi, 1994: 85–158)

CAPITALISM UP, FEUDALISM DOWN

But if modern day capitalism was simply that part of a predominantly agrarian economy in which a few locally produced goods and services were traded for money—and that is certainly how it began—it would never have grown into the dominant way in which the bulk of economic life in advanced societies is now organized. But it did so grow, eventually moving from the margins of economies organized on other lines into the mainstream of general economic life. It did so for two reasons. It did so under the logic of its own processes, as the search for sources of raw materials to process—and for markets in which to sell processed materials—steadily widened over time. It did so too with the growth of first the economic, and later the social and political, influence and importance of the new social classes created by that widening. Capitalism was initially at most a marginal strand in economies because most people working in them were neither capitalists nor the people the capitalists directly employed. Capitalism became the dominant way of organizing economic life as the number and proportion of capitalists and wage laborers grew in first one economy and then another, and as the number and proportion of members of pre-capitalist classes—in the European case, largely feudal landowners and peasantries tied to the land—commensurately declined.

Both conceptually and historically, it is worth differentiating the kinds of capitalists at play in this fundamental economic transition. Historically, the first key group were predominantly *merchant capitalists*—men surviving and indeed prospering by buying cheap and selling dear (or, in American English, by buying low and selling high): initially buying surplus goods from more developed economies on the fringes of Europe and then later, after the opening of the Americas, trading in both metals and commodities, and in peoples **enslaved** to produce both.

However, and from virtually the outset, there were always among the ranks of those merchant capitalists a group of more successful merchants who ultimately retreated from trading commodities altogether, preferring instead to trade in money. These were the early *financial capitalists*—men surviving and even prospering by lubricating that buying and selling process, lubricating it by lending both producers and merchants money ahead of the trade, the better to cream off a fee once the trading was over. And as for the producers themselves: initially they would be either mainly artisans and their guild masters working on raw materials produced locally in the agrarian sector (animal hides, simple metals and the like) or more *commercially minded landowners* (or their tenants) keen to convert at least part of their agrarian surplus into things for sale.

Indeed the emergence of commercial agriculture, and of an agrarian labor force no longer formally tied to the land, was key to the generalized growth of capitalist economic activity in the early modern period: particularly the growth of a wool-producing economy sustaining the emerging textile industries of the Low Countries and the United Kingdom, wool produced from sheep (mainly in England and Spain) that were tended by agrarian workers paid (an admittedly extremely low) wage. The development of large-scale industrial production—the thing we tend to associate most with capitalism as an economic system—actually therefore only emerged late in the day; and for most economies (as Table 1.1 shows) *very* late in the day. Industrial capitalism took off only *after* a long period of increasingly effective agrarian, mercantile and financial capitalism. The industrialist followed the merchant, the commercial farmer and the banker onto the world stage only from the 1750s, just as the factory worker whom the industrialist employed only then followed onto the historical stage the artisan, the enslaved African and the agricultural day laborer.

So one set of distinctions worth bearing in mind as we explore further the emergence and character of capitalism is the existence of differing ways of being a successful capitalist: as a merchant, a farmer, an industrialist or a banker. And another set of distinctions worth keeping alongside those is that between the types of economic system of which capitalism was and is but one.

Table 1.1 Industrialization: W.W. Rostow's "tentative, approximate take-off dates"

Country	Take-off	Country	Take-off
Great Britain	1783–1802	Russia	1890–1914
France	1830–1860	Canada	1896–1914
Belgium	1833–1860	Argentina	1935–
United States	1843–1860	Turkey	1937–
Germany	1850–1873	India	1952–
Sweden	1868–1890	China	1952–
Japan	1878–1900		

Source: Rostow (1960: 38)

Feudalism was clearly, for Europe at least (and, as it happened, for Japan too), historically the predominant other, such that the spread of capitalist ways of organizing economic life necessarily involved the corrosion of feudal ways of doing the same thing. You could not simultaneously be an agricultural day laborer—paid a wage—and a feudal peasant tied to your land. Your transformation into the first necessarily involved your no longer being the second; and yet, to fully understand modern capitalism, we have to grasp that, in Europe prior to 1861 at least, both conditions could and did exist side by side. For just as the more capitalist-advanced economies of Western Europe were shaking off the shackles of a feudal economic and social order in the first half of the seventeenth century, those shackles were being re-imposed in Eastern Europe in what historians now recognize as "the second serfdom." Even on the European landmass, that is, capitalism grew to dominance in different places and at different times. The English slowly recast their countryside over a four-century period—so that by the 1820s all agricultural labor was wage based. The French, by contrast, only removed their feudalism after 1789, consolidating in the process a class of small-scale peasant-proprietors whose presence in the post-Napoleonic French social formation would slow the nineteenth-century rate of French industrial growth; while the Romanovs (the re-imposers of serfdom in 1642) did not even formally abolish feudalism in Russia until 1861.

So capitalism from the outset must be understood, even in its European nursery, as an economic system characterized by combined but *uneven* development. It was not just on the world stage, but also locally, that the relative competitive strengths of various areas of capitalism differed over time. Capitalism emerged most potently where ruling groups were most open to the spread of commercial practices (in certain Italian city-states, the Low Countries and the United Kingdom in particular). It spread more slowly in societies where feudal landowning institutions were more heavily entrenched (particularly in France and in Spain), and even by the middle of the nineteenth century was hardly visible at all in economies in which the restoration of centralized political control had been forged on the basis of a renewed support for a feudal aristocracy (particularly in Russia under the Romanovs). The early heartlands of commercial capitalism—northern Italy and northern Germany—by then lagged behind because of a lack of political unity and (in Germany's case) because of the regular sweep across its commercial heartlands of European armies bent on the destruction of their enemies. Poor Germany was ravaged by religious wars in the first half of the seventeenth century and by the clash of eighteenth-century superpowers that only ended in 1815, leaving nineteenth-century Western Europe as the stage on which industrial development would then spread in waves: first in the United Kingdom (after 1760) and in France (after 1815), then East and South after 1870 into Germany and Italy as each finally formed itself into a united nation-state.

WAVES OF CAPITALIST DEVELOPMENT

The mention of nation-states serves to remind us that the economic changes associated with the rise of capitalism did not occur in a political vacuum; on the contrary, the rise of capitalism and the rise of the modern system of nation-states occurred in parallel. And although this is not a book on the nature of nation-states, a full understanding of the history and character of modern capitalism does require some wider knowledge of the political formations within which capitalist economic relations first emerged and then flourished.

Hence this: the emergence of the European system of nation-states was itself a key element in the break-up of European feudalism. National centers of political authority slowly established themselves in England and France in the late medieval period, and then more dramatically in Spain in 1492 (when the armies of Ferdinand and Isabella drove the last of the Moors off the Iberian peninsula), in Austria in 1566 (when Charles II split the Habsburg dominions into two) and eventually in Holland in 1648 (as Spain conceded Dutch independence). That year, the Treaty of Westphalia officially ending the Thirty Years War also established in international relations the principle of territorial sovereignty on which, by the twentieth century, the entire global order came to be based. Within those national territorial boundaries, one institution—the modern state—came to have a monopoly on the legitimate use of force, and with it a commensurate set of responsibilities: the maintenance of law and order, the regulation of property and trade, the supervision of labor and family life, and the maintenance where possible of a stable banking system and national currency. It was within the legal security of the nation-state that individuals were then able more reliably to accumulate capital, workers were on occasion able to win employment protection, and borrowers and savers were able to establish relationships of mutual trust. Capitalism did not invent the nation-state, but the rise of nation-states was a vital prerequisite to first the regional and then the global spread of capitalism. It was within particular national boundaries (and under particular national laws) that capitalism became the dominant form of economic life in first one nation-state and then another.

Understood as a system of *national* economies, full-scale capitalist industrialization of the kind that created the modern global economy occurred in a series of nineteenth- and twentieth-century waves. Indeed it is possible—in relation to the development of industrial capitalism at least—to talk productively of first-wave capitalisms and of second-wave capitalisms, and to treat recent changes in the global economy as evidence of something we might term a third wave.

In first-wave industrial capitalisms—those which began the process of capitalist industrialization on a significant scale in the first part of the nineteenth century (notably the United Kingdom, the Low Countries, the northern parts of the United States and possibly France)—industrialization followed a relatively lengthy period of internal social differentiation which had already brought about significant shifts from pre-capitalist to capitalist ways of organizing economic activity in key sectors *before* large-scale factory production was introduced. Agriculture was already commercialized. Textile production was already extensively organized on cottage industry lines, and so on. These were the economies that had already evolved a strong commercial and financial middle class, a strong nation-state and a liberal and secular culture. Pre-capitalist ruling groups had already weakened or been replaced in these societies, and rural populations had already settled into wage work as the norm. In these first-wave capitalisms, it was a recognizably modern middle class that then set the direction and pace of economic change, presiding over a nineteenth-century industrialization process whose tempo was, in retrospect, relatively slow but whose reach and penetration into the economy as a whole was relatively thorough and dense from early on.

Second-wave industrial capitalisms—Germany, Japan and even Russia—were rather different. Their industrialization only began on a significant scale in the latter part of the nineteenth century; and here the impulse to industrialization arose less from the internal evolution of their societies than from external pressures working on their ruling groups from an emerging capitalist world order. In these societies, the rise of capitalism to a position of significance, if not dominance—it entirely failed to become dominant in Russia, as we will see—was more or less coterminous with the process of industrialization itself. The move from feudalism to capitalism, and from agriculture to industry, was historically fused rather than being, as in first-wave capitalisms, either entirely absent (as with feudalism in the United States) or separated in time. And as both cause and effect of this process, the pace of industrialization was more rapid and more brutal in these second-wave capitalisms than in the first-wave ones, the degree of peasant and worker resistance was greater, and the middle classes of second-wave capitalisms played a subordinate role to that of pre-capitalist ruling groups in the orchestration of industrial development. Indeed it was the national military needs of these aristocrat-led regimes which often provided the impetus to industrialization. The resulting political culture of second-wave capitalisms was accordingly far more likely to favor strong state involvement in economic management than did the political cultures of economies that had industrialized more slowly and under autonomous middle-class control.

To fully understand the political geography of the second half of the twentieth century, it is also vital to remember that, unlike its German and Japanese equivalents, the Russian late nineteenth-century dash for capitalist industrial growth ultimately failed. It came too late, and was too modest, to match either the German industrialization on Russia's western edge or the Japanese industrialization on its eastern border. The residual weight of Russian feudalism—the size of the Russian peasantry and the absence of any significant middle class—left the Russian army vulnerable to defeat by better equipped Japanese (1904) and German (1914–17) military forces: military forces generated from, and modernized within, societies already equipped with larger and more self-confident middle classes. Those military defeats then sent Russia off into a series of revolutions that eventually left Bolsheviks in power in Moscow, Bolsheviks who subsequently industrialized their Soviet Union without passing through any conventionally understood capitalist stage. In the guise of the Communist Party of the Soviet Union, the Russian state stood in for/actually replaced the Russian middle class as an industrial modernizer, and from the 1930s forced through a rapid military-industrial development, the social horrors of which only became generally known after 1956 when Nikita Khrushchev's "secret speech" first exposed the realities of unbridled Stalinism. Nineteenth-century Europe had possessed only one model of industrialization—a capitalist one—but the twentieth century now had two. It had a capitalist one whose growth performance seemed to stall in the two decades immediately following World War I, and a state-socialist one that lifted Russia into great power status again by 1945. It was the clash between those two which then underpinned an entire Cold War, one that only ended with the unexpected collapse of the Soviet Empire in 1989 and of the Soviet Union in 1991.

STAGES OF CAPITALIST DEVELOPMENT

It is hard to pull back into view now the dominant mind-sets of the Cold War years, when it was not obvious to anyone how the Cold War would end, or indeed if (short of the mutually assured destruction of a nuclear holocaust) it would ever end at all. But it is worth remembering that between 1945 and 1991 Soviet leaders regularly claimed that eventually state-socialist economies would out-produce capitalist ones, and that their claim was equally regularly refuted by critics of centralized economic planning and communist political tyranny. That in the end the critics won, and did so in such a convincing manner, speaks volumes about the superior dynamism over time of economies organized on capitalist lines. It is a dynamism over time which is best grasped by understanding the various stages through which well-established capitalist economies inevitably run. For, from the very inception of industrial capitalism, the unavoidable competition between capitalists, and between capitalists and those they employ, necessarily changed—and changed more than once—the internal landscape of each major capitalist economy in turn; so that the history of each is best grasped as a series of stages that capture the particular capital-capital, and capital-labor, accords prevalent in each.

Scholars have varied in the labels used to describe those stages while broadly agreeing on the existence and timing of stages as such. Some scholars have developed a timeline separating "proprietary capitalism" from first "managerial capitalism" and then "collective capitalism," focusing on the characteristic size of companies and the structure of their management. (Lazonick, 1991) Some have preferred to split that timeline into "pre-Fordist," "Fordist" and "post-Fordist" stages of capitalist development, focusing on the way production is organized inside capitalist factories (Aglietta, 1979); and still others have written of "liberal capitalism," "monopoly capitalism" and "state monopoly capitalism," focusing on the changing nature of government-business relations over time. (Jessop, 1990) But regardless of the detail of the labeling used, the very act of splitting the timeline of fully developed capitalist economies into distinct stages reflects a widely shared recognition, among many economists and economic historians, of the need to *periodize* the development of capitalism, the better to understand how and why capitalism works now.

The different periods through which fully developed capitalisms have moved to date are very clear in the case of the US economy, and we might use that as an exemplar of the general capacity of capitalism, as it develops, to qualitatively alter itself internally.

Early industrial capitalism in the United States, as indeed in all the core industrial capitalisms, was initially characterized by the fierce competitive struggle of small firms, each employing few workers and deploying what we would now think of as relatively primitive technologies. The productivity of labor was largely tied to the physical strength of the laborers themselves, supplemented only by simple machinery powered by steam and coal. By the 1890s, however, that was giving way to the emergence of large corporations capable of mobilizing vast quantities of financial **capital**. These were corporations prepared to use that capital to develop more sophisticated machinery increasingly driven by electricity, and corporations prepared to deploy professional managerial staffs to capture larger and larger shares of ever expanding national and global markets. Where the total output of each small firm was modest in the first half of the nineteenth century, the total output of the large corporation was anything but small by the first half of the twentieth century. Indeed by as early as 1908 Henry Ford had developed the semi-automated production line method of car assembly that came to bear his name—**Fordism**—and capitalism's basic problem had begun to shift away from an inability to produce in volume toward one of needing to find adequate markets for a volume of output whose complete sale was vital to corporate profits and corporate employment. It was a balance between output and sales that the American economy managed to achieve for a while during the Roaring Twenties, but it was a balance which was entirely missing through the years of the Great Depression which followed.

The scale and scope of North American and European unemployment in the 1930s serves to remind us—as we will see more fully in Chapter 5—that even in its most developed centers in the United States, Western Europe and Japan, full-scale industrial capitalism has been capable of raising the living standards of the majority of its citizens *only* in the very few decades that divide us from the end of World War II. Prior to 1939, living standards for most industrial workers in most industrial economies were extremely modest by modern standards, and only slightly improved in the 1930s from those commonplace a half-century earlier. Since 1945, however, living standards have soared for most people in most fully industrial societies. They have not soared for everyone. Poverty remains a serious issue for at least one American in seven as this volume is drafted; but that relative poverty is one that is now *not* shared by the other six in seven. On the contrary, their living standards have effectively more than doubled since the end of World War II, in line with moves toward generalized affluence that have occurred in all the core capitalist economies that began their industrial development as small-scale liberal capitalisms a century or more ago.

Since 1945 America has known two long periods of sustained economic growth, each of which has transformed the living conditions of modern Americans. The first period, broadly from 1948 to 1973, was one based on the productivity growth associated with the generalized application of Fordist methods of assembly line production. In that first period, the competitive dominance of American manufacturing kept employment high in the car plants of the American Midwest, and strong trade unions among American car workers made sure that at least part of that productivity came back to their members in the form of higher pay and benefits. Not all sections of even the American economy flourished in that fashion—living standards in the still largely rural American South certainly did not—but for a generation a combination of rising productivity and output, corporate profits and union wages, spread standards of life hitherto known only by the professional middle classes *out* into the American suburbs and *down* into blue-collar America itself. When that productivity growth stalled in the 1970s, and after a decade of relatively stagnant growth and living standards in the 1980s, a second period of rising consumption came to America. This second "Reagan-inspired" growth period, up and running by 1992, was based on rising productivity again—this time, rising productivity largely generated by the generalized application of computer-based technology to one American economic sector after another—but the prosperity it generated was not based as before on rising wages/hour. Instead, as in the United Kingdom, governments of a Center-Right persuasion broke the power of trade unions in the 1980s, allowed income and wealth inequality to grow apace for more than three decades, and presided instead over a period of rising consumption that was primarily underpinned by longer working hours, the rise of the two-income family, and the spread of personal credit and debt. It was that Reagan/Thatcher growth period that then crashed so dramatically in the financial crisis of

Table 1.2 The stages of American capitalism

Competitive capitalism (1860s–1898)	*Corporate capitalism (1898–1939)*	*Regulated capitalism (1939–1991)*	*Transnational capitalism (1991–)*
Small business competition in local and regional markets	National-level competition among large corporations (trusts)	Large US corporations extend their reach and are dominant in global markets. SEC regulates financial markets	US-based and other transnational corporations compete in all major world markets; global outsourcing
Strong craft-based unions in some industries. Extensive workplace control by skilled workers	Employers are dominant, labor weak and/or illegal; corporate paternalism & company towns in some sectors, open conflict in others	Labor unions are legalized, increase membership, and become important players in wage-setting and politics. NLRB established; "labor accord"— real wages rising with productivity	Labor accord ended; global mobility of capital increases its bargaining power over labor; union membership falls; inequality between workers and employers grows
Limited government; military and police functions; land policy; tariffs; canal building; subsidies to railroads	Federal Reserve System is established to regulate money supply and banking system	Macroeconomic stabilization through deficit spending, expansion of social security, medical, unemployment and other insurances	Weakening of regulations; slowing of the growth of government spending; steps toward global governance through autonomous institutions (IMF, WTO)

Source: Adapted from Bowles *et al.* (2005: 161) (copyright Oxford University Press: reproduced with permission)

2008, producing a generalized global recession from which both the US and UK economies were still struggling to free themselves half a decade later.

The pattern and dating of successful and unsuccessful growth periods do vary by economy. The German timeline is not quite the same as that of the United States. Japan's periods of boom and bust differ from both; and we will trace and explain those variations in the next chapter. But what we need to note here—before we explore local differences—is the extent to which all capitalist economies share the two great vulnerabilities that are visible in that US story, vulnerabilities that drive capitalism from stage to stage. They share the vulnerability of each other, in the sense that each national economy needs to out-compete the rest, and yet increasingly needs the rest to be sufficiently successful to at least consume levels of imports that can sustain the export sector of each economy in turn. And they share the vulnerability of capitalism's core internal class contradiction, namely the need of each individual firm to keep its costs (and particularly its labor costs) down, while simultaneously requiring strong wages in other firms that both weaken their relative competitiveness and provide a source of effective demand for the products of the original company. Those two vulnerabilities then speak to a third: the propensity of capitalism as a system to experience periodic crises of output and employment that are ultimately rooted in capitalism's central fallacy of composition, namely that the wage-containment that is good for an individual firm is not necessarily always good for firms taken as a whole.

The very dynamism of capitalism as a way of organizing economic life explains its capacity to replace all other forms of economic organization over time. But that same dynamism builds an inherent instability into capitalism as both a global system and as a set of national economies. There are those—we will meet their arguments in Chapter 4—who feel that the instability at the heart of the capitalist growth machine is best left unmanaged, to be understood and endured as the necessary price of a way of organizing economic activity that has been, and continues to be, historically transformative. But there are others—we will also meet their arguments in Chapter 4—who think that, on the contrary, the instability associated with capitalist growth is too endemic and too arbitrary in its impact to be simply ignored; and that accordingly the central economic task of democratically elected governments is that of managing the system. But both sides agree that what you inevitably get with capitalism is economic growth *and* economic instability, side by side. Since the instability is the consequence of the growth, that leaves us with the core question of whether instability can be managed without choking off growth itself. The answers to that core question will no doubt continue to differ, but the question itself will not go away.

THE CHARACTER OF MODERN CAPITALISM

The unexpected collapse of the Soviet Union at the end of the twentieth century left capitalism as the only viable growth model available to would-be industrializing nations, and opened the way to a third wave of industrial development—a wave bringing the standard forms of capitalist economic life to a wider and wider range of national economies. The ubiquity of capitalism with which this chapter began is in that sense of very recent origin, the product of the collapse of state socialism on the one side and of the rapid global deployment of modern forms of capitalist production on the other.

As recently as 1945, it made sense to think of capitalist industrialization as something occurring only at the *core* of the emerging global system. True, Japan was always an outrider (parts of South America were another): one whose outrider status we will explore in the next chapter. But otherwise capitalist industrial development was largely restricted to what we might term the core industrial rectangle: a narrow geographical space running from Chicago to Moscow along its northern edge and maybe from Baltimore to Milan along its southern equivalent. If you wanted to be part of industrial capitalism, you had to migrate into that rectangle; and millions of people did exactly that in the last half of the nineteenth century and in the quarter century that followed the end of World War II. Indeed, and for an entire generation after 1945, the world was accordingly divided economically into a *First* World of fully industrialized capitalist economies, a *Second* World of state-socialist economies less fully developed and industrialized than their capitalist competitors, and a *Third* World of colonies and former colonies that were hardly industrialized at all. But no longer: labor migration has now been trumped by the global migration of capital itself. South Korea industrialized as an American client state—and did so with clear military-government leadership and US financial assistance—even before the Iron Curtain fell; and when that curtain did fall, when the Second World reverted back to capitalist ways, the global flows of private investment funds then helped to rapidly and extensively industrialize whole new areas of the global system. These new areas include Brazil, Russia, India and China—the so-called BRIC economies—two of which had been under-developed capitalisms for a century, and two of which were state-socialist societies now reverting to a capitalism which their previous communist leaders had falsely claimed to have permanently left behind.

Of course, painting the history of an entire global system with so broad a brush has its limits and its costs. There is a whole Latin American story of blocked economic development to weave into the mix, had we but the time and space. (Haber, 1997) Argentina was the tenth richest economy on earth in 1914, ahead then in per capita income of economies such as France, Germany and Italy that are now among the most successful of all. (*Economist*, 2014) Mexico and Brazil grew as rapidly as did Japan in the first decades after World War II; and in both sets of examples, private enterprise was linked to state support (and even, in the two post-war cases, to conscious policies of **import substitution industrialization** (ISI) that broke decisively with the **free trade** maxims so favored by more fully developed capitalist powers). But in general, industrial capitalism until the fall of communism was fully developed only in parts of the global economy, and in predominantly "northern" parts at that. The global system as a whole was characterized not simply by combined but also by uneven development, and large swathes of the globe remained organized economically on non-capitalist lines.

Economies were capitalist in that global order only where the main means of production were *privately owned*. That private ownership was and is now largely corporate—capitalist economies dominated by private firms that are professionally managed—

though sectors remain where capitalist firms are sufficiently small as to be directly managed by the very men (and occasionally women) who own them. Economies were and are capitalist where production is wholly focused on the creation of *commodities*—goods and services to be sold—and where the motive of both production and sale is the pursuit of *profit* for the company owning the resources being processed and sold. And economies were and are capitalist where the actual work required to produce commodities is done by people who *sell their labor power* to the firms owning the means of production. In a fully capitalist economy, those actually making the products that later are sold do not own the raw materials they work on, the tools they use in the production process, or the products that their labor generates. All these key elements in the cycle of production and exchange remain the private property of the company or individual employing them. What the vast majority of people own instead is their own ability to labor. In capitalism, labor power itself becomes a commodity. In a fully capitalist economy, it is the sale of their labor power—the exchange of their work for a wage or salary—which enables them to buy the products of other people's labor in order to survive themselves; and it is those wages that constitute the consumer power on which the corporations overseeing the production ultimately rely for the sales (and profits) which alone keep them in business. *In an economy organized on capitalist lines, that is, you get private ownership, profit seeking, commodity production and the sale of labor power;* and in an economy organized on capitalist lines, you get an interlocking system of dependence between workers and their employers on the one side and between those employers and their workers as consumers on the other.

FOR FURTHER EXPLORATION

This is not the first text to attempt such an overview. For others, see Fulcher (2004), Saunders (1995), Berger (1986), Wallerstein (1983), Lippit (2005), Centeno & Cohen (2010) and Meltzer (2012). On the history and emergence of capitalism, see Braudel (1982, 1984) and Mielants (2007); and for its contemporary character, start with Gamble (2014) and then see Bowles et al. (2005).

NOTE

1 Terms in bold in the text are explained more fully in the Glossary.

2

CAPITALISM FROM ABOVE

As we will discuss more fully in the last chapter, there are many ways of judging the success of contemporary capitalist economies, and some of those ways are more controversial than others. But whenever that judgment is made, and pretty well regardless of the metric used, it is striking that not all capitalist economies do equally well. That in its turn then suggests that not all such economies are exactly the same; and indeed they are not. Some are particularly successful if you measure their performance against criteria of international competitiveness or rates of economic growth. Some are particularly successful if you measure them against a measure of GDP/head, or against a set of welfare criteria (including the happiness of the people within them). Some are particularly successful if you measure them against all four sets of such criteria, and some aren't particularly successful no matter how they are judged. And that differential performance seems to matter now more than once it did. For when the Cold War still pitted capitalist economies against state-socialist ones, all the capitalist economies scored well in the comparison, and there was very little academic chatter about variations of performance within the capitalist bloc itself. But more than two decades later, with that Cold War competition long gone, it is now the variation in the performance of different capitalisms, rather than the superiority of capitalism per se, that commands public attention and invites scholarly response.

VARIETIES OF CAPITALISM

This variation in performance between major capitalist economies is currently clearest in two very different dimensions of economic life—trade performance on the one side and worker rights on the other. If you stack economies up by their ability to earn more from their exports than they pay for their imports, you will find that some very big economies run trade deficits year by year that never seem to go away. (There are big global imbalances between creditor and debtor nations these days, imbalances that are now deeply embedded.) In the last three decades an excess of imports over exports has certainly been the condition of both the US economy and the British: both now run deficits that they finance by borrowing heavily from abroad, using highly developed sets of financial institutions for that purpose. Other economies, by contrast, run substantial trade surpluses: Germany for one and China for another. Now whether China, as currently the world's largest producer of manufactured goods, is actually a proper capitalist economy is a question which we will soon need to settle. But what we can already say is that, no matter what kind of economy it possesses, China currently does not perform well in comparative terms when the metrics in play change: when the focus shifts, for example, from trade balances to levels of welfare provision or degrees of worker rights. Then the star performers are found elsewhere. They include a series of small Scandinavian economies, and again the German one, but neither the Chinese nor the American. If you are a full-time employee in the United States and also pregnant, currently all you enjoy is a statutory right to 12 weeks of unpaid maternity leave without loss of job, under legislation that treats pregnancy as a temporary disability! If by contrast you are similarly fully employed and pregnant in Norway (where, as it happens, per capita income is currently higher even than in the United States), your job is guaranteed as you take up to 13 months of maternity leave paid at 80 percent of your current salary or 46 weeks paid at 100 percent; and you and your partner can additionally each take up to 2 weeks of paid leave if subsequently your young child becomes ill. Capitalisms clearly vary in what they achieve in economic terms and what they offer in social ones.

There is now a considerable academic literature on this variation in economic and social performance, a literature replete with typologies that seek to capture the core differences between the major national economies that are organized on capitalist lines. The first attempts at differentiating types of capitalism often split economies simply into two. Michel Albert, for example, in an early piece of writing that was very influential in its time, differentiated an "American model" (and not an "Anglo-American model" since UK welfare provision was still far too European in the 1980s) from a "core European" model that was, for him, a mixture of Rhine capitalism and Alpine. For Albert, "the neo-American model was based on individual success and short-term financial gains; the Rhine model, of German pedigree but with strong Japanese connections, emphasizes collective success, consensus and long-term concerns." (Albert, 1993: 19) In that early formulation, the choice came down in the end to one between America and the rest—a choice then reformulated a decade later, by Peter Hall and David Soskice, into one between **liberal market economies** (LMEs) and **coordinated market economies** (CMEs). And by then, the United States and the United Kingdom had been grouped together (as LMEs, alongside Australia, Canada, New Zealand and Ireland) to be compared to a group of ten CMEs that included all four Scandinavian ones plus the Netherlands, Austria, Germany and Japan. (Hall & Soskice, 2001: 19)

The Hall and Soskice LME–CME distinction has dominated the academic conversation about models of capitalism for more than a decade now. (Coates, 2015b) The distinction uses the term **liberal** in its European, not American, sense, meaning by it not progressive or social democratic but rather anti-statist and conservative. So LMEs are ones in which major firms rely on pure market relationships in their dealings with other firms, with their labor force and with their sources of finance. In LMEs, firms hire and fire workers on a regular basis, depending on immediate market conditions. They borrow and repay money after relatively brief periods of time; and they select and change their supplier companies to maximize their short-term profit and dividend yields. In CMEs, by contrast, major firms handle those critical relationships through a greater reliance on non-market means of coordination. They build strong networks linking firms, banks and workers together in longer-term relationships based on high levels of mutual trust. The Hall and Soskice argument is broadly that each way of running a capitalist economy is equally viable—European networked capitalism is likely to be just as competitive over time as its American rival—but that more hybrid models (those mixing the defining features of both LMEs and CMEs) are likely to fall victim to economies organized on more consistent lines.

The basic distinction between LMEs and CMEs has been—and remains—important politically as well as academically, acting as a counterweight within both the academy and the public square to those many conservative voices on both sides of the Atlantic which argue for the inevitable superiority of purely market-based forms of capitalism. To those voices, to those arguing that Europe can no longer afford a generous welfare state, the continuing economic success of a quintessentially CME such as Germany has provided defenders of welfare provision with strong counteracting evidence. But that is not to say that the basic distinction between LMEs and CMEs is problem free. It is not. When, for example, you label the United States as an LME you imply that *all* of the leading sectors of its economy rely on short-term market relationships with their suppliers and their consumers, and so push out of view those sectors whose long-term profitability is closely tied to government agencies, federal subsidies and public regulation: arms producers, the oil industry, agriculture and pharmaceuticals to name but four. And by grouping economies together, you imply high levels of similarity that might quite simply not be there. Putting Germany and Japan into the same category is a case in point. Both have strong network relationships between firms and their sponsoring financial institutions, but they have very different sets of worker rights and very different kinds of labor movements, which is why other scholars have preferred to develop typologies which are basically triangular in shape, so allowing Germany and Japan to be differentiated from each other while keeping both conceptually distinct from the United States.

THREE KINDS OF CAPITALISM

Such typologies tend to differentiate *three* kinds of capitalisms: those in which private sector actors are relatively free of government regulation and strong labor codes; those in which, by contrast, governments and their industry ministries play an important leadership role; and those in which strong sets of worker rights, fixed by both collective bargaining and supporting legislation, set limits on the freedom of employers to hire and fire. Triangular typologies of this kind constitute a diagrammatic response to the recognition that the central question at the heart of a capitalist economy—who actually decides how investment, production and employment are to be organized—varies on two axes rather than simply on one. The autonomy of private firms to do their own thing depends both on the degree of state regulation over private capital, and on the strength of labor rights in the face of the private ownership of the means of production. And since these powers and strengths are perpetually in dispute between leading economic and political actors, the actual placing of individual capitalist economies within the triangle is likely to both vary over time and rarely, if ever, occupy a polar position.

Given the complexity and volatility of the basic power relationships operating within capitalist economies, a triangular representation of ideal types (allowing for a scaling of position along each dimension of the triangle) seems to work better as an explanatory device than a simple binary distinction can ever hope to do. The left face of the triangle can measure the power of labor against capital. The right face can measure the power of capital against the state. The base of the triangle can measure the extent to which the state is responsive to the power of labor; and each point of the triangle can capture a particular mind-set dominant in the wider society into which the economy is inserted. So that as we rotate the triangle, different political ideologies and associated value systems then come into view: **classical liberal** ideas when we get to market-led capitalisms, **social democratic** views at more consensual capitalisms, **conservative**/nationalist ideas when the capitalism is state led. As we drop down the triangle from top to bottom, the number of stakeholders tends to widen and income inequalities tend to diminish; and as we

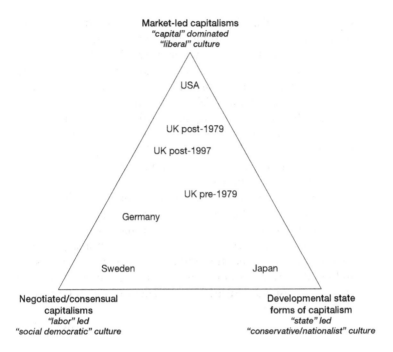

Figure 2.1 National models of capitalism

move across the triangle from right to left, the distribution of social power tends to even out.

What the diagram then suggests is that, in ideal, typical:

- *Market-led capitalisms*, investment decisions lie overwhelmingly with private companies, who are left free to pursue their own short-term profit motives and to raise their capital in open financial markets. In such capitalisms, workers enjoy only limited statutory industrial and social rights, and earn only what they can extract from their employers in largely unregulated labor markets. State involvement in economic management is largely limited to market-creating and protecting measures; and the dominant understandings of politics and morality in the society as a whole are individualistic and classically liberal in form.

- In *state-led capitalisms*, by contrast, investment decisions are again primarily seen as the right and responsibility of private companies, but those decisions are invariably taken only after close liaison with public agencies, and are often indirectly determined through administrative guidance and bank leadership. In such capitalisms, labor movements tend still to lack strong political and social rights, but there is space for forms of labor relations which tie some workers to private corporations through company-based welfare provision. The dominant cultural forms in such capitalisms are likely to be conservative and nationalist.

- In *negotiated* or *consensual* capitalisms the degree of direct state regulation of capital accumulation may be still small, but the political system entrenches a set of strong worker rights and welfare provision which gives organized labor a powerful market presence and the ability to participate directly in industrial decision-making. The dominant cultural networks in these capitalisms are invariably social democratic or Christian-democratic ones.

(Coates, 1999)

In such typologies, the post-Reagan United States and the post-Thatcher United Kingdom are both normally positioned close to the less regulated point of the triangle. Japan in the immediate post-war decades, and South Korea in the last quarter of the twentieth century, are normally positioned close to the "state-led" point of the triangle. The Scandinavian economies are firmly anchored close to the "strong labor movement" point, with West Germany nearby. For those building such a three-fold typology, the need now is to position China—as an economy that was until very recently communist but which is currently creating a powerful private sector that is heavily state directed. Here the issue is whether China should join Japan and South Korea within the triangle, or whether the triangle should be converted into a quadrilateral with China (and perhaps Russia) positioned as economies that are rapidly coming to capitalism from communism rather than (as in the majority of the other cases) economies that have come to capitalism from some now long-gone feudal past. Designing typologies to capture the variety of capitalisms becomes more complicated, that is, more varieties of capitalism emerge that have to be captured inside the typologies so designed!

CREATING THE VARIETIES

All this typological innovation makes sense and has value only because, and to the degree that, individual national economies emerged in the twentieth century sharing common capitalist characteristics set amid different institutional forms; and they did. The varieties of capitalism we know now are predominantly post-World War II creations, each a complex product of the interaction of two main things: their own prior economic development, and the global settlement called into being under American leadership in the immediate aftermath of first Nazi Germany's surrender and then that of Imperial Japan. It is a creation story with which we all need to familiarize ourselves if we are ever fully to understand the nature of our contemporary condition.

The *United States* emerged from World War II as the globe's leading industrial power, and the one least disturbed by the ravages of war. Troubling as it might be to say, World War II was actually beneficial to the US economy. For in addition to the war ultimately destroying two major competitor economies (the German and the Japanese), the original wartime mobilization brought full employment back to an economy still struggling to shake off the Great Depression, and the demands of war production transformed America's manufacturing base. That base was transformed from one held back in the 1930s by lack of demand into one that throughout the war years acted as a veritable "arsenal of democracy." The end of hostilities might well have tipped the US economy back into recession again, as wartime demand was terminated; but in the event it did not. That was partly because wartime demand was not fully terminated: military spending remained a large and significant element in the post-war American economy after 1945, as it does to this day. (Kidron, 1967) But recession was avoided too by the spending of the accumulated wages of returning soldiers, and by the wage demands those soldiers placed, as reconstituted industrial workers, on major American corporations in the immediate post-war years.

As we saw earlier, the enormous productive capacity built up for war between 1941 and 1945 was redirected after 1945 into the production of consumer goods sold to unionized American workers and their families, in an historically unprecedented combination of rising private corporate profits and rising northern male living standards. (D. Gordon, 1994) For at least three decades after the end of World War II, the US economy combined large and competitive privately owned companies manufacturing consumer goods with a government-sustained military-industrial complex and a large and growing white middle class. It was a combination of rising consumption and continuing military spending that kept American factories humming with economic activity for a generation, and helped establish *market-led* American capitalism as the model to be emulated by ruling groups in every other aspiring capitalist economy.

That emulation of all things American by governing elites elsewhere in the capitalist part of the divided post-war global order was particularly clear in the two major economies whose military had been defeated by the force of Allied arms: Germany and Japan. Initially, post-war Allied concerns were focused on avoiding a repetition of German and Japanese militarism by keeping each occupied-economy weak relative to the rest. But as the Allies quickly divided into the hostile camps of the Cold War, the parameters of the possible for the defeated Axis powers dramatically widened. West Germany by the time of the Berlin Blockade in 1948 and Japan after the Chinese communists defeated Chiang Kai-Shek in 1949 found themselves as frontline states in the new global division of power between Washington and Moscow. Paradoxically, the reconstruction and enhanced competitiveness of the economies of America's recent bitter enemies then became a vital US concern. Accordingly, those in power in Washington DC used their brief period of military occupation not to deplete German and Japanese capitalism as they had initially intended, but instead to reconstruct strong manufacturing sectors whose internal institutional arrangements were significantly different from those prevalent in America itself. In the broadest sense, as the United States retreated in the late 1940s from its New Deal and wartime enthusiasm for partnership between capital and labor, it used its military dominance abroad to orchestrate New Deal-type economic and social settlements first in West Germany, and then in Japan.

In *West Germany*, the social forces and institutional structures necessary to that reconstruction were already well in place. Wartime bombing had, of course, leveled factories and cities, and the loss of life among German soldiers and civilians had been enormous; but even so the basic economic and social infrastructure of a successful industrial capitalism remained firmly in place. What was gone from the German political and economic stage was the credibility and legitimacy of the officer class and the institutions of Nazi terror. What had emerged as potentially stronger from the war was the civilian side of the German economy: its big manufacturing firms with their close relationship to their sponsoring universal bank; the small and medium-size enterprises (the *Mittelstand*) that had been such a feature of the pre-Nazi German economy; the strong trade unions that the Nazis had only temporarily crushed; and an education system that included a strong vocational training sector. Post-1945, all these elements fused together into a particular West German model of capitalism—one characterized by some commentators as a form of "organized capitalism" (Chandler 1990: 335) and by its own leading politicians as a unique "social market economy." It was a model of capitalism characterized by *co-determination* (big firms answering to supervisory boards on which both banks and workers were strongly represented), *managed labor markets* (big firms not being free to simply hire and fire at will) and high levels of *mutual trust* between economic actors bound together by sets of legal requirements and shared social understandings. United by a common desire to rebuild Germany in the wake of the wartime devastation, successive German governments, business corporations and labor unions combined to generate a German "economic miracle" in the 1950s, the decade in which in the West German economy "the growth of manufacturing output averaged 10 percent per annum, and GDP 8 percent per annum." (Brenner, 1998: 66) It was a growth performance that left West Germany by the 1960s back in play as an internationally successful capitalist economy—one combining rising wages with relatively low levels of income inequality. The ratio of high wages to low ones was at least one-third lower in West Germany by the 1970s than it was in the United States, and the ratio of CEO pay to average wages probably 60 percent lower (Streeck, 1997), and yet the model clearly worked. Indeed the volume of German exports actually exceeded that of the United States in 1972, for the first time in the post-war period. (La Barca, 2013: 42–3)

In *Japan* the post-1945 economic changes initially overseen by occupying US military forces were similar, but still distinct and unique. Even more than in the German case, pre-war Japanese economic development had been driven by companies networked together around a common bank, companies that prospered by out-competing other networked companies and by offering lifetime employment guarantees to at least some of their core employees. The linkage of these *zaibatsu*, as they were called, to the Japanese military in the 1930s initially tempted US policy-makers to break these networks up, as part of the American attempt to demilitarize the defeated Japanese state. But post-1949, other geo-political imperatives took precedence, and so slowly a revitalized Japanese version of capitalism emerged with American blessing. It was one built around a set of highly successful networked companies (now known as *keiretsu*) offering lifetime employment and welfare guarantees to their core workers (maybe one Japanese worker in four) and in receipt of strong economic leadership from the demilitarized Japanese state. In the 1950s the newly re-established independent Japanese state used the Ministry of International Trade and Industry as its key policy tool, one emulated later by other struggling capitalist economies, not least the United Kingdom and France. The Japanese labor movement (in the form of independent unions) was defeated in a series of unsuccessful strikes in the early 1950s, so that Japanese post-war growth—unlike that in Germany—came to be based initially on the long hours worked by Japanese employees rather than on any high wages they might have earned, and so was more dependent than its German equivalent on successfully selling Japanese products to better paid workers abroad, mainly in the United States. In 1979, American workers toiled on average 1,834 hours a year. Their Japanese counterparts toiled 2,129 hours (Mishel et al., 2009: 364), a gap—equivalent to more than seven 40-hour weeks per year—which helps explain why and how, like the West German economy, the post-war *state-led* Japanese economy also had its period of remarkably rapid economic growth. For Japan, the growth figures are even more striking than those for West Germany—"between 1950 and 1960, Japanese manufacturing output grew at any average annual rate of 16.7 percent, and GNP at about 10 percent—the highest rates among the advanced capitalist economies" (Brenner, 1998: 79)—to leave the capitalist bloc of economies led by the United States in possession of at least three highly successful economies by the end of post-war capitalism's golden years of expansion (1973), and no longer of just one.

The capitalist economy that struggled most to recapture its former international competitive strength was that of the United Kingdom. British capitalism had been the dominant manufacturing power in the second half of the nineteenth century, but had surrendered that position to American capitalism by 1945 and to both German and Japanese capitalism a generation later. A hybrid of all three basic capitalist models, the UK economy post-1945 combined strong financial institutions and a military-industrial complex left over from its imperial heyday with an emerging civilian manufacturing sector and strongly entrenched trade unions. The temporary post-war dislocation of both the German and Japanese economies gave the United Kingdom one last decade—the 1950s—in which its average living standards were second only to those in the United States, but thereafter (and in spite of repeated government attempts at different economic growth strategies) the United Kingdom's hybrid model of capitalism slipped down one international league table of economic performance after another. The United Kingdom remained a member, but no longer the strongest member, of a select group of economies that collectively constituted the core of the post-1945 capitalist global order. All of them experienced sustained economic growth right through to the 1970s; and in the process, all of them transformed the living standards of the vast majority of their citizens. It was this capitalist club—led by the United States, but including the economies of Western and Northern Europe, the white dominions of the British Empire (Canada, Australia and New Zealand) and Japan—that spent the first three decades of the Cold War years prospering internally, and creating in the process a recognizable gap between their living

Table 2.1 Comparative economic performance in the capitalist core

	1938	1948	1960	1970	1980	1988
Western Europe	83.2	56.5	65.7	73.5	103.0	91.4
North America	121.6	149.3	137.0	127.4	98.6	109.7
Australia & NZ	134.4	84.6	67.4	76.3	81.7	67.0
Japan	20.7	14.5	23.2	52.1	76.3	117.9
Weighted average	100.0	100.0	100.0	100.0	100.0	100.0

Note: The figures represent GNP per capita in each region divided by the per capita of the three top regions taken together times 100. Western Europe consists of the Benelux and Scandinavian countries, West Germany, Austria, Switzerland, France and the UK. North America is the USA plus Canada.

Source: Arrighi (1991: 43, 45)

standards and those prevalent elsewhere in either the Second World or the Third.

THE THREE WORLDS OF WELFARE CAPITALISM

So it is possible to tell the story of post-1945 capitalist development in the years of the Cold War as one dominated by the emergence in the global "North" of three different kinds/models of capitalism. But we should note too that there was one other "type of capitalism" much discussed once the Cold War was over, when the focus of academic attention shifted away from the choice between capitalism and socialism to one between varieties of capitalism. That other type was one that had also quietly emerged in Northern Europe during the years of American–Soviet competition, one that had developed particularly in *Sweden*, a type that people outside Scandinavia tended to treat as a unique form of "welfare capitalism."

This growing sense of Scandinavian exceptionalism was not unwarranted, since there were features of the social, economic and indeed political settlement slowly created in Sweden after 1945 (and to a lesser extent in Denmark and Norway) that were not generally replicated elsewhere. Partly those features were political in origin. Unlike other leading capitalist economies, Sweden from 1932 to 1976 was governed by an unbroken series of Center-Left governments that set high priority on both full employment and social equality—governments which orchestrated a "middle way" for the country between totally unregulated capitalism on the one side and extensive state ownership of industry on the other. In a classical piece of class compromise, in 1955 Sweden's social democratic government adopted what it termed a *solidaristic* wage policy. This was one in which, across the economy as a whole and via complex negotiations between the national federations of both labor and capital, similar wage rates were paid for similar jobs, regardless of the ability of individual firms to pay. That kind of wage-solidarity meant that inefficient firms found their wage bills inflated and their competitiveness undermined. There were no easy sweatshop routes to profitability for poorly performing Swedish firms. But the unemployment resulting from their loss of market share was acceptable to trade unions in Sweden (indeed such unemployment was a deliberate part of the policy) because the government also pursued *active labor market policies*. That is, Swedish governments financed the retraining of displaced workers and helped with their relocation costs as Swedish labor moved from low-productivity employment to high-productivity work, in the process keeping Swedish unemployment rates among the lowest in Europe. Moreover and from the 1960s, successive Swedish governments (including more Center-Right ones after 1976) supplemented such novel labor market policies with the construction of what was, by comparative standards, a remarkably generous set of welfare programs: including high-quality health care and childcare services, sickness benefits and pensions, many designed to help married women with children return to paid work. And yet the Swedish economy, for all its welfare spending, still managed to stay internationally competitive. Seventeen of the largest 100 multinational corporations in the 1970s were head-quartered in Sweden—big names such as Volvo, Saab, Electrolux and IKEA—even though the Swedish economy was by then sustaining rates of personal taxation (and a size of government spending as a proportion of GDP) that were well in excess of those common even in Germany, let alone in America, the United Kingdom and Japan.

How the Swedish economy got away with it, and why Sweden should have settled into such a capitalist model, then stimulated the creation of a new set of typologies—this time ones generated not by mainline economists or by political scientists so much as by sociologists: students of poverty, gender and welfare. The defining moment in that comparative welfare literature came in 1990 with the publication of Gósta Esping-Andersen's hugely influential *The Three Worlds of Welfare Capitalism*. Esping-Andersen differentiated "liberal" welfare capitalisms from "conservative" ones, and differentiated both from "social democratic" welfare capitalisms of the Scandinavian kind. In the process, he drew attention to key dimensions of capitalist economies on which we will focus more attention in the next chapter: namely the differing ways in which such economies create, reward, train and develop their labor forces, and the associated ways in which they support those sections of their populations excluded for a variety of reasons from participation in paid labor. Welfare provision by the state is only one way of making sure that people without wages survive in capitalism—that provision is always supplemented to some degree by support from family members, voluntary organizations or private companies selling welfare services. But modern welfare states vary, Esping-Andersen argued, by the degree to which—in the choice between the state and the market—they make people buy welfare services from private providers rather than distribute them free of charge at the point of use. They vary, that is, by the degree of **commodification** common within them, and by the degree to which the right of access to those services is, or is not, universal.

- In *liberal welfare capitalisms*, for example, publicly provided welfare provision tends to be limited in generosity and residual in nature—available only to those unable to afford the better quality services provided by the private sector. In such welfare states, services such as higher education and the insurance to cover health care costs are regularly bought and sold like any other commodity. Accordingly general levels of taxation tend to be low by comparison with other forms of welfare state, and public sector employment correspondingly limited.
- In *social democratic welfare capitalisms*, by contrast, publicly provided welfare provision tends to be generally available and of high quality. Health care is normally free at the point of use, and higher education is free or heavily subsidized. In

such welfare capitalisms, it is privately provided welfare services which tend to be residual, taxation levels which tend to be high, and public sector service employment which tends to be correspondingly large.

- In *conservative welfare capitalisms*, access to publicly provided welfare services tends to be by category and status, and not to extend to services designed to undermine traditional gender roles. Taxation levels in such welfare states tend to outstrip those in liberal ones, but to settle at a lower level, and to support fewer public sector service workers, than in fully functioning social democratic welfare states.

What the existence of this and similar typologies underscores is the degree to which welfare provision has become a common feature of all modern capitalist economies—and understandably so. For once ordinary workers had been fully separated from the land by the development of industrialized towns and cities, their ability to survive and prosper turned entirely on their access to a regular wage: such that exclusion from wage labor for whatever reason immediately produced serious hardship and generalized despair for any worker so afflicted. As this was recognized more and more in the last decades of the nineteenth century, ruling groups in each emerging major industrial economy began to experiment with modest forms of welfare provision (and to do so normally as a way of heading off industrial and social protest), starting first with industrial injury compensation, then with sick pay and with pensions, and eventually with unemployment insurance. In every case, coverage was initially very modest and restricted to just a few categories of workers (normally men, normally unionized). But in the wake of World War II—and in large measure because of the mass mobilizations and hardships caused by that war—generally available basic welfare services were put in place across the industrialized world by governments regardless of their political stripe. This time these welfare services included mass free education for children of teenage years, basic pensions for older workers, and generalized health care for most if not all societal members. Again, initially, standards of provision across all the industrialized capitalisms were modest, in line with the modest living standards common everywhere in the 1940s, but eventually rising affluence in the 1960s brought another round of welfare expansion—this one designed to bring welfare programs more into line with the quality of life associated with rising private wages and salaries.

Which particular kind of welfare capitalism was first established in the 1940s and extended later depended primarily on the kind of political party in charge of its design. In the late 1940s in the United States, as the enthusiasm for New Deal-type governance wilted, even Democratic presidents were unable to pass universal health care coverage through increasingly conservative Congresses. What they could win, however, and did win every twenty years or so, was health care (either free at the point of use or heavily subsidized) for different categories of Americans: for veterans in 1944, for the old and the poor in the 1960s, for children in the 1990s, and for the near-poor through the Affordable Care Act introduced from 2010. By contrast, more social democratically led political systems did establish universal health care—in the UK in 1948, in Sweden in the early 1950s—and in the latter case at least oversaw from the 1960s a significant increase in the range and quality of services that collectively constituted a **social wage** to supplement the private one, particularly a social wage enabling married women with children to build their own careers without carrying the dual burden of unassisted childcare. Christian democratic-led countries such as West Germany and Italy also provided steadily better benefits for the sick and disabled, for the old and for the temporarily unemployed. Where they struggled— in ways in which Scandinavian welfare states did not—was with welfare policies easing the entry into the paid labor force of married women with children. Female participation rates in paid labor grew everywhere in advanced capitalism from the late 1960s—two-income families becoming increasingly the norm— but the rates of female labor market participation were significantly higher in predominantly Protestant Northern Europe than in the continent's predominantly Catholic South.

VARIETIES UNDER CHALLENGE

Each of these ways of linking welfare provision to core capitalist processes came with strengths and weaknesses. The great strength of liberal welfare capitalism was (and remains) how little residual welfare provision costs either in terms of personal taxation or as overheads on employment. Welfare retrenchment in the United States in the 1990s certainly went hand in hand with rapid job creation, and many of those now advocating further cuts in welfare benefits regularly point to that decade in support of their case. Its great weakness, of course, was (and is) that people on welfare in liberal welfare capitalisms such as the United States do tend to stay poor. Welfare carries a stigma, and the system has few mechanisms for breaking cycles of deprivation. Poor areas tended to generate and then regenerate poor housing, poor schooling and at best only poorly paid employment. Liberal welfare regimes rarely close income and wealth gaps; indeed they are more likely to widen them.

At the other extreme, by contrast, social democratic welfare capitalisms of the kind developed in Scandinavia avoid many of those weaknesses, but the price of that avoidance was and is high. Levels of personal taxation in Sweden have come down over time, as they have across capitalist economies as a whole: electoral pressures to curb welfare spending have grown everywhere. But those taxation levels are still higher in social democratic regimes even than in the rest of the European Union, and the danger always remains in generous welfare systems of healthy people of working age permanently avoiding paid work by surviving on welfare substitutes.

Conservative welfare capitalisms still occupy some middle ground in the Esping-Andersen vision. They combine strengths of universal coverage for things such as health care, unemployment, pensions and temporary sickness with avoidance of the very high levels of personal taxation characteristic of welfare systems of the Scandinavian variety. But they too have weaknesses, at least from a progressive point of view. In conservative welfare capitalisms, the rights of women are not fully reinforced in the manner of social democratic ones—older, more traditional views of gender roles still prevail. And in a recession, the price of protecting those in work by guaranteeing them semi-permanent job security is paid by young workers unable to break into employment, and by consumers denied access to low-price goods from retail outlets open for long hours on every day of the week.

So for clear and understandable reasons, there is still an on-going debate in both the academic literature and the public square about the desirability of different forms of welfare provision. It is not a debate that is likely to end any time soon, but it is a debate whose character is now beginning to change. It is beginning to change because, regardless of the precise form that welfare provision took in the many varieties of capitalism which developed in the post-1945 period, the scale and character of that provision is now under increasing challenge across the system as a whole. It is under challenge because of the very success of welfare provision itself. It is also under challenge because of the problems of global competitiveness now faced by the capitalist economies on which those welfare states are based.

There is a real sense in which welfare states in the post-World War II period were ultimately too successful for their own good. Certainly the improved quality of health care provision had an enormous impact on the shape and size of national populations in all the advanced capitalisms, reducing childhood death rates at one end of the population spectrum and raising the average age of death at the other end. Moreover, post-war improvements in access to, and in the quality of, education at both secondary and college level eventually created a more highly educated labor force. It was a labor force a larger and larger percentage of whom were women educated as well as or better than men. That change alone set in motion huge transformations. It not only helped raise the productivity of labor. It also triggered among other things—as we will see in more detail in Chapter 5—a significant fall in birth rates among families in which increasingly both adults were engaged in full-time paid employment. Welfare systems in advanced capitalisms were initially consolidated after 1945 in a world that was characterized by an entrenched global North/South divide that kept manufacturing in the North and the scale of service employment there low. They were consolidated in northern societies dominated by patriarchal patterns of work and reward that made the "male breadwinner model" the norm, sustaining living standards that were at best modest for most people most of the time. Those same welfare societies today face an economic and social landscape that is entirely different. Living standards are higher, and expectations of what constitutes an adequate minimum are higher with them. Patriarchy is now widely challenged, and the traditional form of the family is no longer all-pervasive. Low-productivity service work has replaced high-productivity manufacturing industry as a major employment source in most core capitalisms; and the global international division of labor is in flux. Add to that, this: that in the most affluent of the advanced capitalisms at least, the "baby boomers" born in the immediate wake of World War II are now not only retiring in increasing numbers. They are also refusing to die off at the rate and at the age of their parents. They are lasting longer, and facing a generation of workers which is in consequence proportionately smaller in the overall population. The ratio of workers to pensioners in the US economy in 1950 was 16:1. It is now nearly 2:1 (Spriggs & Price, 2005); and because it is, the longevity of the baby boomers is currently triggering fierce political debates—within and between generations—about who should carry the burden of both rising health care costs and the provision of adequate pensions.

The fierceness of that debate is also a product of the growing problems of competitiveness now being experienced by the developed capitalist economies on which existing welfare states are based. Welfare spending can be financed relatively easily when rates of economic growth are high, and when everyone who wants a paid job has one. But from the 1970s onwards, growth rates in advanced capitalist economies began to slow, competition between them began to intensify, and levels of involuntary unemployment in many cases began to creep up. The contemporary "crisis of the welfare state" was a crisis of unemployment, poverty and competitiveness even before it became a crisis of demography. The crisis of competitiveness struck different national capitalisms at slightly different times. The United States struggled with stagnation and inflation (stagflation) in the 1970s but not in the 1990s. By then, both were gone. West Germany struggled with unemployment more in the 1990s than in the 1980s, in part because of German unification; and is struggling still with low levels of labor market participation by young workers and with the spread of low-paid employment, the so-called "mini jobs." (Solow, 2008: 14) Japan's economy stalled in 1992, and has been struggling with problems of deflation pretty consistently ever since. Sweden struggled with economic growth and job creation in the 1980s, but bounced back a decade later. The UK economy actually went through 63 quarters of unbroken economic growth from 1992, its longest unbroken run ever. It was a run that ended only with the general financial crisis of 2008. The varieties of capitalism came under challenge, that is, partly because of internal weaknesses in each variety, and partly because of more fundamental weaknesses developing in the linkages between them.

So it is possible—and in a full study it would be vital—to examine each major economy in turn, but for our purposes here it is the general processes at work in this most recent period of capitalism on which we ought more properly to dwell. The most fundamental underlying storyline has to be one about—of all things—labor productivity. Ultimately, living standards can only rise for everyone if the general productivity of labor is rising. Rising living standards require workers to produce more per hour than they did before, so that there are more things being made or services provided for people to consume. That rising productivity was achieved prior to the 1970s partly by moving labor from sectors of low productivity to sectors of high (the Swedish solution—mainly effected elsewhere by moving people from agriculture to industry). It was achieved partly by generating full employment (the **Keynesian** solution—more people working, giving more people money with which to buy). But it was primarily achieved (as we first saw in Chapter 1, and will see again later) through this thing called Fordism—by creating manufacturing industries based on semi-automated production lines that replaced the sweat of the human brow with the steady hum of the assembly line. (Coates, 1995: 22–7) It was the exhaustion of the productivity leap created by the dissemination of Fordist modes of production through one manufacturing sector after another that brought the post-war period of steady economic growth in the advanced capitalist world to an end in the 1970s.

It took a while to find a new source of productivity growth. The generalized application of computer-based technologies would do that job from the 1990s. But while the search was on, competition intensified between advanced capitalisms for a greater and greater share of what was by the 1980s an only slowly growing economic cake. The Japanese economy felt the first impact of that intensified competition. The willingness of US policy-makers to allow Japanese manufacturers—especially car manufacturers—to capture more and more of the American home market diminished in the 1980s, as rust belts opened up across North America; and the United States still had the global power then to impose a re-valuation of the Japanese yen—which it did in 1986. The so-called Plaza Accord—negotiated between Ronald Reagan's Treasury Secretary and his Japanese and German counterparts—forced a dramatic re-valuation of both the German and the Japanese currency, making their exports significantly more expensive in the American domestic market. The German economy, less dependent on US markets than on European ones, rode out the storm. The Japanese economy did not. Its governments dramatically expanded demand at home to cross-compensate for the loss of export markets, in the process sparking a financial bubble (particularly in property prices) that eventually burst in 1992. The Japanese economy has been in search of a route back to high levels of economic growth ever since.

It was the US economy that bounced back most in the 1990s, creating more than 20 million new jobs, in part by attracting into its financial system large quantities of investment funds from overseas—particularly Japanese-based investment funds. These were funds owned by institutions and people who increasingly lacked confidence in the stability and competitiveness of America's leading European and Asian competitors. The flows became in that sense, and for a while, self-fulfilling. America flourished, and other economies did not, because the United States attracted mobile foreign direct investment whose distribution was simultaneously a cause of, and a response to, the combined but uneven economic development of the global system as a whole. For the other feature of the post-1970s global capitalist order that set it apart from its predecessor order in the 1950s and 1960s—the feature that coincided with the arrival of computer-based productivity growth—was the enhanced international flow of capital. Controls on the movement of capital across national boundaries that had been laid down after 1945 were progressively dismantled in the 1980s as part of the deregulatory strategies advocated in the United States by Ronald Reagan and in the

United Kingdom by Margaret Thatcher, and were then rendered mute by the arrival of the computer and the Internet.

In consequence, capital flowed abroad; and as it did so, it began to undermine the competitive viability of high-tax welfare capitalisms of the Swedish, and even the German, variety. It made sense for national governments to pursue a high-wage, high-tax, high-productivity economic growth strategy if their major companies were dependent on home-based demand and were prepared (or obliged) to reinvest their profits in home-based production systems. But as capital was freed to move off-shore, high wages and high taxes quickly became a disincentive to investment at home. Better, from the point of individual firms, to seek low-wage production platforms abroad. True, there was still the need to find someone elsewhere who was paid well enough to buy the final product—or at least to find markets financed by rising private debt—but that was a problem for the system as a whole, not for the individual firms that made it up. What might have been rational at the level of the national economy became irrational at the level of the individual firm, so that either side of the millennium, whole welfare systems built on the premise that capital would not go off-shore increasingly struggled to sustain essential public services as manufacturing investment did in fact leave, as wages stagnated, and as electoral tolerance for high taxation stagnated with them.

THE MORE THINGS CHANGE, THE MORE THEY STAY THE SAME?

This greater global mobility of capital was already creating a new international division of labor before the unexpected fall of communism transformed things yet again. In the last years of the Cold War, a string of Asian "Tiger" economies had unexpectedly broken through to higher levels of investment, growth and living standards, so that a world so rigidly divided after 1945 into a First, a Second and a Third World had begun at the margins to change. South Korea, Taiwan, Hong Kong and Singapore all recorded rapid rates of economic growth in the 1970s and 1980s. (Deyo, 1987; Gereffi, 1990: 10) The annual average compound growth rate for the Taiwanese economy between 1960 and 1996 was

8.3 percent, for South Korea it was 8.1 percent. (van Ark & Timmer, 2002)

The South Korean growth story from the 1960s in particular was both unexpected and transformative. It was unexpected. The South of the peninsula after the Korean War seemed the least likely place for successful capitalist industrialization; and yet that industrial transformation did eventually occur. It occurred under American political leadership and economic tolerance. The development of the South Korean economy under tight direction by its political elite was encouraged by Washington because of South Korea's geo-political position as a frontline capitalist state facing the most Stalinized of the communist satellites; and it was fueled by the steady injection of first American and then Japanese capital. South Korea benefited from a Japanese state-led growth strategy that involved locating off-shore (in economies such as South Korea) low-productivity Japanese industrial production—initially things such as textiles. Then after the Plaza Accord, the South Korean economy benefited from a string of joint ventures with Japanese companies keen to locate production outside Japan and free of a strong yen. In the process, South Korea joined Japan as a clear example of state-led capitalist development. Its state agencies played a key developmental role. Its internal corporate structure was similar to that of Japan—called *chaebol* in this case rather than *keiretsu*—and it adopted the same initial treatment of labor: long hours and low wages. Average working hours in South Korea in the 1970s and 1980s, as the economy first established itself in global markets as a supplier of ships and cars, were excessively long by global standards: averaging 54.7 hours a week as late as 1980. That number has come down slightly of late, but the relative positioning has not changed. South Korean workers labored 2,256 hours per year on average in 2008, according to the **OECD**, as against, at the other extreme, 1,389 in the Netherlands and 1,764 across the OECD economies as a whole. (Rampel, 2010) Working conditions characteristic of European and North American industries in the late nineteenth century were replicated in South Korea in the late twentieth, in a pattern of dependent development that saw South Korean firms slip-streaming behind Japanese ones as both rapidly built up industrial capacity at home and markets overseas.

This rise of the Asian Tiger economies was hailed by proponents of free market capitalism as clear evidence that under-development was not an inevitable consequence of exposure to stronger and already fully developed capitalist economies. The counter view—that development in the North was based on, and served to reproduce, under-development in the South—had by then justified the adoption, across parts of South America in particular, of policies of ISI. These sought to create an internally strong manufacturing base by building big protective walls to keep out cheaper and more technologically sophisticated northern-made products. ISI had triggered rapid economic growth in places such as Brazil and Mexico in the 1950s and 1960s. As we briefly referenced in Chapter 1, the Brazilian economy expanded at an annual rate of 6.8 percent between 1951 and 1980. The Mexican equivalent rate was 6.4 percent. (Pinheiro et al., 2004) But by the start of the new millennium ISI growth strategies had been largely abandoned as the protective walls surrounding ISI were brought down by trade agreements such as **NAFTA**. (Franko, 1999: 52–75) In consequence, and by the century's end, significant flows of capital were moving around globally not just between advanced industrial economies in the North but also into and out of developing economies in both Asia and Latin America. It was into that already turbulent mixture that from 1991 onwards a collapsing communist system then added the extra ingredient of a Second World, once closed to capitalism, now unexpectedly also open to this global capitalist embrace.

Before turning to that crucial shift, however, we must note one other feature of this growing globalization of capital flows; and that is its relationship to the other great global flow that had fueled capitalist industrial development over time: namely the global flow of labor. As we briefly noted at the end of Chapter 1, prior to the development after 1991 of a string of newly industrializing economies collectively labeled as the BRICs—Brazil, Russia, India and China, and you might also add Indonesia—if people wanted to participate in factory-based wage labor, they had had to move to do so. Factory employment didn't come to them. They went to it. Indeed they went to it in huge numbers. Every major industrial take-off required internal labor migration— a huge move of people from agriculture to industry and from country to town—and many take-offs had been accompanied also by a significant movement of people from agricultural work in one country to factory work in another. The biggest nineteenth-century migration story associated with the rise of industrial capitalism is the movement of 20 million people—mainly but not exclusively from Europe—into the United States between 1871 and 1910 (Briggs, 1996: 55); and that migration itself had followed the earlier forced migration of predominantly African peoples as slaves into the American South: both into the South of the United States and into South America itself, not least into Brazil. Post-1945, with that international migration closed off, the United States settled into another migration story: first of African-American rural workers moving from the American South into northern cities in search of factory employment; then of Cuban and Asian immigrants arriving as political refugees; and finally of steady flows of Hispanic immigrants—some arriving legally, others not. The European equivalent is a story of migration into Europe after 1945 of people from former colonies (from North Africa into France, from South Asia and the Caribbean into the United Kingdom) plus guest workers flowing into West Germany from Turkey once the building of the Berlin Wall in 1961 had stopped the migration of East Germans there. In total and in consequence, by the year 2000, across the globe as a whole, maybe one human being in every thirty-five was an international migrant—someone working and living in a country other than the one in which they had been born. (Wolf, 2003)

That migration didn't end with the collapse of communism, but it definitely changed. It changed in part because now workers from the former Soviet Union began to move around inside the European Union, a pattern of migration which steadily intensified as one former Soviet satellite after another formally joined the European Union. There was and is now an internal EU labor migration story to add to the mix; but in terms of scale it is a migration story that pales into insignificance when set against its equivalent in China itself. For the internal reforms orchestrated initially by Deng Xiaoping in the wake of the death of Mao freed as many as 180 million Chinese peasants to move from rural poverty to the promise of better wages in the emerging industrial cities in China's eastern-most provinces. In the space of a single generation, the number of people seeking paid work—the size of the global **proletariat**—doubled; and the number of them earning poverty wages grew commensurately. This is a story to be told in more detail in Chapter 3; but it is worth remembering now that as recently as 1980 more than 40 percent of the population of the developing world was still surviving on less than one dollar a day. (Dollar, 2004) Capitalism may eventually generate affluence, but it invariably starts cheap.

The majority of those migrants were at that point in China. The internal transformation of China has been, and remains, a carefully managed affair. The Chinese Communist Party had watched the sudden collapse of the Soviet Union after Mikhail Gorbachev unsuccessfully tried to orchestrate incremental change from above, and clearly decided that it wanted the change without the collapse. So bit by bit, the Chinese Communist Party allowed the development of private enterprise within China. Bit by bit, it allowed the entry of foreign capital; and bit by bit it exposed large state corporations to both managerial autonomy and market competition. The result has been the creation in China of a new form of capitalism—one that for political reasons cannot admit its name. Politically, a Marxist-justified political structure has to be post-capitalist; but economically China is engaged in a movement which in Marxist terms is "history going in reverse"—going from communism to capitalism rather than going from capitalism to communism. Bit by bit, that is, sections of the Chinese Communist Party are turning themselves into an industrial owning class, creating a form of capitalism that analysts have begun to label as "networked" or "*guanxi*" capitalism. (McNally, 2007)

It is a form of capitalism characterized by a mixture of private and public enterprises, the private ones operating still as yet without a clear set of property rules, and both sets linked together by networks of connections, finance and shared technical knowledge. It is a form of capitalism in which the Chinese Communist Party leadership uses its control of the banking system to direct investments to projects and priorities that it favors; and it is a form of capitalism that grows by exporting manufactured goods to more affluent economies abroad. It is also a form of capitalism that is hugely successful. China is now officially the world's leading manufacturing economy. It is poised to become the world's largest economy overall, and it currently runs a trade balance with the other capitalist giant—the United States—of an unprecedented scale. The US trade annual deficit with China in 1991 was $10.4 billion. It is now over $300 billion. Not that everything in the Chinese economy is, in capitalist terms, wonderful. Far from it: as a still emerging capitalism, and one with an enormous population—one in six human beings is currently Chinese—China's GDP/head puts it only in the second league of capitalist nations; and the speed of its growth masks a

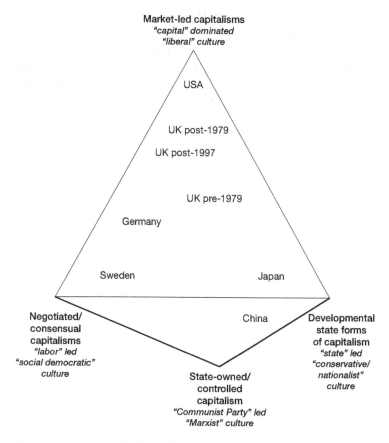

Figure 2.2 National models of capitalism updated

series of internal weaknesses that may yet come back to haunt it. Indeed because those are weaknesses that potentially might impact us all, we will review them briefly in the last chapter. But for the moment we need note only this. That currently we have a new hybrid form of capitalism in play—one combining communist political rule with capitalist economic practice. Our earlier triangle does indeed need resetting as a quadrilateral. Four main types of capitalism now fill the globe, and it is their interplay which will shape the future of the world.

FOR FURTHER EXPLORATION

On varieties and models of capitalism, start with Hall & Soskice (2001), then go to Coates (2000, 2015b), and to Ebanau et al. (2015). On welfare capitalism, the two best sources are Esping-Andersen (1990, 2002) and Pierson (2001). On China, begin with Hutton (2006), then go to McNally (2007).

3

CAPITALISM FROM BELOW

The very term "capitalism" necessarily pulls our attention upwards, toward those who own and deploy the thing at the core of the term: namely "capital." It is therefore so easy and so normal to see capitalism from the top down, and to tell its story as one of the rise and fall of particular capitalists, of particular capitalist economies, even of particular capitalist classes. We ourselves have done this at least twice in this volume already: tracing the emergence of a combined but uneven global capitalist economy by discussing the relative strengths of particular capitalist classes in different national contexts; and explaining and characterizing the role of the Russian and Chinese communist parties as modernizing agencies standing in for (actually substituting themselves for) missing capitalist middle classes of the more conventional kind. If we were to stop now, you might be forgiven for thinking that the only social actors in play in the story of capitalism were middle classes (**bourgeoisies** as the French would have it) and the other pre-capitalist dominant classes (aristocracies of various kinds) whose power those middle classes ultimately eroded.

But capitalism always comes with two basic classes, not simply one, and so indeed did feudalism. The feudal aristocracy might in some sense have "owned" the land, but they did not thereby work it. A far larger class of peasants tied to that land did the actual planting, growing and harvesting of the crops which then sustained the feudal aristocracy in their more privileged lifestyle. Even the small-scale master craftsmen who provided the predominantly agricultural economies of feudal Europe with the simple tools that agriculture then required had their artisan apprentices who worked with them and under their supervision. And when feudal agriculture gave way to commercial capitalist agriculture, the feudal peasantry did not somehow vanish into mid-air. It was instead transformed (often very painfully for the people caught up in the transformation, as we will soon see) into a paid agrarian labor force who still did the bulk of the planting, growing and harvesting of crops (and the tending of the animals) that were subsequently transported away for sale.

Likewise, as industrial capitalism emerged and came to dominance, the driving force of that change was not simply the factory owners who commissioned and sold the industrial goods that their factories generated. The other driving force were the men and women they employed—the emerging industrial workforce who actually made the goods on a daily basis—men and women whose needs and aspirations were no less real for being normally largely hidden from public view. The story we have told thus far of the rise and variety of capitalism can therefore be told again—and indeed needs to be told again if its full complexity is to be understood—but this time *told from below,* told as the history of the men and women who labored long and hard to produce the goods and services characteristic of capitalist output at its various stages of development. To the history of capitalism told from the perspective of the capitalists who control it, we need to add the history of capitalism told from the perspective of the workers they employ—from the perspective, that is, of the men and women who do not control it.

In fact, telling the story of capitalism that way helps underscore what is probably the most important feature of our present condition, at least for those of us concerned with issues of social justice and human happiness—namely the layered nature of contemporary global capitalism. Right now capitalisms that are old and well-established (such as the United States and the United Kingdom) and capitalisms that are new and emerging (such as Brazil and China) co-exist and interact daily on the global stage for the very first time. Each sits alongside the other; and as they do so, it matters to the competitive interplay between them that the labor conditions prevalent within each vary in significant and crucial ways. In the broadest sense as we will soon see, the labor conditions of early capitalism (early capitalisms in the past, and capitalisms that are emerging now) were and are particularly unpleasant, while those of older and more mature capitalisms were and are less demanding. Each advanced capitalist economy still does have its dark underside—poverty wages for one worker in three in the United States, super-exploited Turkish guest workers in Germany (G. Friedman, 2010), and so on. But still, for the broad mass and generality of working people in fully developed capitalisms, both wages and working conditions are far better now than they were in the distant past, and far better now than they are for their contemporary equivalents in developing capitalisms.

In consequence, what is currently going on—in the sphere of labor rather than in that of capital—is a competitive struggle between, on the one side, established capitalisms with mature labor conditions and, on the other, capitalisms so early in their own emergence that their labor conditions are far less sanguine. Indeed, whether the latter drag down the former—whether we are collectively engaged in some global race to the bottom in terms of wages and working conditions, or in some global race to the top—is one of the key issues of our age, maybe even ultimately *the* key issue; and it is impossible to fully grasp its contemporary nature and importance without a clear understanding of capitalism's labor conditions both early and late. Hence this chapter.

CREATING THE EARLY WORKING CLASS

If any one thing is already fully clear from the early chapters, it is possibly this: that the transition from feudalism to capitalism in Western Europe and Japan did not occur overnight. Nor did it occur at the same time, or with the same speed, in each national context. The transformation was slower in first-wave capitalisms than in second-wave ones; and the later the transformation occurred, the more rapid and severe was its initial character and impact on the agrarian and urban workers unfortunate enough to be caught up in it. The transformation was slowest and longest in the United Kingdom, later and faster in Germany and Japan, later still and initially less successful in first Russia and then China. But for all the variation in speed and origin, once the industrial form of capitalism began to emerge, the social changes going on beneath the surface of economic life, and the working conditions of the men and women caught up in them, showed remarkable degrees of similarity over time and place.

Because the movement from feudalism to capitalism was slowest in the United Kingdom, the British story helps us to see in slow motion things that happened more rapidly later elsewhere; and so can act as a kind of template for the changes associated with the emergence of capitalism everywhere. And in this regard, the key thing to note, in the British case at least, is that the "industrial revolution" that produced the United Kingdom's first factories really got underway only after 1760 and only became extensive after the development of railways from the 1820s. It got underway, that is, only at the very *end* of a long historical transformation of non-agricultural production from simple artisan-based workshops into (initially) larger work units—factories—which were themselves (later still) transformed into modern industrial plants by the development of new technologies designed to increase the productivity of factory-based labor. That long and slow transformation of industrial production was accompanied by two others, equally prolonged. It was accompanied by the centuries-long change of the rural economy from a predominantly subsistence to an exclusively commodity-producing one, with lots of people driven from the land as feudal holdings were enclosed into separate commercial farms. And it was accompanied later—in the long century dividing the Treaty of Utrecht in 1713 from the Congress of Vienna in 1815—by the capture by UK-based merchants (supported by their navy) of a larger and larger share of the growing world trade in basic commodities and slaves.

So the producing classes in the British experience of capitalist transformation were not therefore initially factory workers. Indeed and as late as 1830, only a very small fraction of English wage earners worked in factories, and even fewer in factories of any scale. The producing classes of early British capitalism were day laborers in an English countryside transformed by enclosure into a fully capitalist agriculture. They were slaves in Caribbean sugar plantations, and they were artisans and home-based textile workers linked to emerging home markets by a growing merchant class. The death of the peasantry, the destruction of an independent artisan class as factory production undercut the price of the goods they manufactured by hand, and the rise and fall of cottage-based workers in the key textile industry that was the first to move into factories on any scale: these were all lengthy processes that occurred in sequence in the English case. They were all lengthy processes that overlapped, if they did so at all, only in the decades of the 1820s and 1830s—coming together then to create the Victorian factory-based working class that we now all recognize as a truly modern workforce.

The factory-based workforces of later industrializing capitalisms were similarly created. They too were the product of displaced peasantries, destroyed artisans, and (often) starved-out, home-based workers in their early textile industries. What later industrializing economies did was not somehow avoid these painful processes of social change and class creation. Rather, what they did was to compress processes that in the United Kingdom had taken centuries into changes now occurring within one (or at most two/three) generations, making the social change more rapid and more brutal still for the ordinary people caught up in the transition.

But whether slow or fast, for the majority of people previously engaged in pre-capitalist forms of production the change was invariably a painful one. It was a painful one for those working in the countryside, and it was painful for those (who were sometimes the same people later in their lives) working in the new factories. In the countryside, the main losers were invariably the poor sections of the feudal peasantry. It was poorer peasants in particular who were robbed of their communal land rights, marginalized within the emerging agrarian capitalist economy, and forced by their lack of access to land and food to sell their labor power. They ended up selling it to more successful commercial farmers; selling it to merchants offering raw materials for processing with simple machinery at home; and selling it to the new industrialists congregating rural labor in factories, first in the countryside and then in the town. Within those factories, or in the systems of cottage-based production or agrarian day labor which accompanied them, life for the early generations of wage-workers was then necessarily high on effort and low on reward. For capital accumulation in the early circuits of industrial capital relied on a particularly *adverse effort-reward bargain*. It required long working hours. It required intensive work routines (indeed the move from cottage to factory was largely prompted by that need to intensify the work process). It required the full mobilization of all forms of labor (men, women *and* children); and it mobilized them as whole family units by paying wages at the very margin of human reproduction. Starvation wages, long hours, no relief from work and struggle: the early working-class experience was truly one of unremitting toil, extensive exploitation, and dreadful conditions of life and leisure.

The first generations of the labor forces of industrial capitalism found themselves caught up, that is, in what both Adam Smith and **Karl Marx** called the process of *primitive accumulation*. (Marx, 1867) They found themselves caught up in the making of a new—and for capitalism, a formative—social class, namely the working class: witnesses in their own lives and experiences to the early emergence of the basic social relations of production that were and remain defining of capitalism. Of necessity, that process was corrosive and ultimately destructive of the social relationships of production that had been dominant prior to capitalism's arrival, and impacted profoundly on the social relations underpinning other forms of social life, particularly those family relationships vital to the daily reproduction of life itself. Capitalism as a mode of production, that is, emerged in a complex relationship with non-capitalist modes of an agrarian and a domestic type. Early capital was accumulated by buying cheap and selling dear, and by extracting profit from wage labor by working that labor long and intensively for the minimum of wages. There was nothing glamorous about early capitalism. It was a system created by blood, toil and sweat: the blood of captured slaves, the unremitting toil of paid labor, and the perennial destruction of the viability of independent producers in both countryside and town.

A CLASS UNITED? A CLASS DIVIDED?

Socially, the early working-class condition was therefore necessarily one of flux and transformation, one in which fully proletarianized workers (those dependent for their daily survival on the payment of a wage, however inadequate) were initially only a *minority* among the producing classes as a whole. Such workers were invariably surrounded by large pre-capitalist social classes. Indeed the later the industrialization, the larger those pre-capitalist groupings were likely to be. Early working classes emerged into a world still full of aristocrats and peasants. They emerged into a world in which (in ruling circles way beyond them) struggles for power, prestige and dominance were the order of the day—struggles between those aristocracies and the emerging owners of commercial, industrial and ultimately financial capital. Capitalists and workers emerged, of course, together. Both were new. B oth were seen as threats to pre-existing modes of life and power; and both emerged as internally fractured social formations. For within the emerging working class itself, the early stages of capitalist transformation established deep (and often politically significant) internal cleavages, cleavages created initially by the very different routes taken by wageworkers into their new proletarian condition.

Those routes differed both geographically and occupationally, and established divisions that were both ethnic and industrial. They differed geographically by the varying distances traveled by first-generation workers from countryside to town. Within the emerging core of the global system and wherever a local peasantry was available for immediate deployment as wage labor, the scale of labor migration was generally limited and ethnic differentiation accordingly small. But in the United States, where no such peasantry was immediately available, local capital accumulation actually required the shipping in of slaves and later the borrowing of foreign peasantries—eventually drawing to the emerging American capitalist industrial machine huge numbers of immigrants displaced within their own economies and societies by the arrival there of agrarian capitalism and intensified political repression. "Give me your tired, your poor, your huddled masses yearning to be free, the wretched refuse of your teeming shore," the Statue of Liberty declaimed; and in the last quarter of the nineteenth century, ruling classes across the semi-periphery of the emerging global system (from Russia and Poland in the East of Europe to Italy and Spain in the South) were only too ready to oblige. The American labor force was, in consequence, more ethnically fragmented from the outset than was normal elsewhere in emerging industrial capitalisms; and American working class unity was thereby more difficult to achieve than would be the case among early working classes in the rest of the emerging global system.

Not that the achievement of unity was easy even in labor forces less divided by ethnicity, language and culture than was the American, for everywhere the occupational routes taken to full proletarianization were always different (and difficult) for different sections of the emerging working class. Some early factory workers came the *rural route*, as displaced agrarian workers who initially often kept strong links back to family and kin in the agrarian economy. Others came as former *domestic outworkers*, workers who had for a period avoided a full dependence on paid labor by buying and selling raw materials and finished products to a local merchant class; and yet others came as *former artisans*, independent workers whose skills and livelihoods had been threatened (and eventually undermined, sector by sector) by the emergence of factory-based production systems. And within those new factories, new skill differentials were then created or won, so that sections at least of the new generations of wage labor came to exercise a degree of autonomy and work control denied to (and often exercised against) the rest of this emerging factory labor force. Within the new factories, that is, the late nineteenth century witnessed the emergence within the expanding working class of what came to be termed "an aristocracy of labor," a more privileged stratum within a broadly unprivileged class. And it was unprivileged: a class of men and women toiling ceaselessly just to sustain a standard of living that barely exceeded what today we would recognize as abject poverty.

The "labor aristocracy" dimension of early working-class formation would eventually be both economically and politically important, because it was predominantly from these new skilled workers that the institutions and leadership of working-class struggle would invariably be drawn. For even newly skilled workers were not free from market pressures and employer resistance as capitalism developed. On the contrary they, more than other sections of the emerging working class, were vulnerable to another tendency that is seemingly endemic to capitalist production—the rhythm of skilling and deskilling that is still so evident today. (Braverman, 1974) Think of basic computer skills now—so general across modern labor forces that they hardly count as a skill at all, but just two/three decades ago the monopoly of the fortunate few. Likewise with the engineering skills of the pre-1914 labor aristocracy: theirs were newly acquired skills that were then quickly and systematically eroded over time to cheapen their labor also. Early capitalism created no safe and fixed spaces for anyone, skilled or otherwise. Just the reverse, really: everywhere as industrial capitalism developed, there was social change, social insecurity, the destruction of old social patterns and networks of support, and the emergence of new ones. And everywhere, there was a lack of clarity about who eventually would be the main casualties of the rapid and profound economic changes underway—a lack of clarity about who would win through and who would not. (Thompson, 1963) Socially, the new working classes emerged, that is, scarred by the divisions and differences of their old conditions, and yet forced into an uneasy unity by the shared degradations, insecurities and exploitations of their new ones.

RESPONDING TO EARLY CAPITALISM

Changes of this scale and severity inevitably invite resistance, and there was plenty of resistance around in the early days of capitalist industrialization. The collective memory of the first generations of day laborers and factory workers invariably contained visions of life before capitalism. Its total rejection (in favor of some preferred golden past) made sense for some, at least in those first generations, in part because initially no one knew for certain if capitalist ways of organizing economic life would actually last, let alone come (as they eventually did) to drown out all their alternatives. Later generations of workers—broadly, anyone working from about 1880—lacked that collective memory, because by then industrial capitalism was visibly here to stay. Then the debate in labor circles turned rather on whether capitalism needed to be simply endured or reformed or replaced by some post-capitalist way of organizing economic and social life that was more modern still. The resistance to the severities of early capitalism remained, but the politics which that resistance sustained began to change.

Industrially and politically, the struggles of early workers were directed to the establishment of independent working-class collective institutions and voice, struggles that were characterized everywhere by intense resistance to any form of working-class organization both by immediate employers and by the state (no matter which dominant class—old or new—controlled that state). The agenda which faced early working-class industrial and political activists was thus an agenda of *representation*: a struggle (or more properly a protracted series of struggles, many often unsuccessful) to have their right to articulate working-class interests accepted as legitimate and permanent by local employing classes. Industrially, the key struggles were those directed to the establishment of trade unions, and to the winning of rights of collective bargaining, initially on the most restricted range of issues (those directly concerned with immediate wages and working conditions). Politically, the key issue initially was the right to vote, the winning of a full democratic franchise: at the outset just for white male workers, but eventually for women workers and for workers of color other than white (white is also a color, of course!). Around that democratic struggle (both before a full franchise was won, and then when it was newly in place) early working-class political activists faced (and debated among themselves) issues of organization and alliance. They debated whether the working class should organize politically in new parties, or subsume themselves within already existing middle-class ones; and if new parties were to be created, whether they should privilege or reject electoral politics. And they sought to create and maintain alliances with related classes in struggle, debating whether the politics of those alliances had of necessity to be radical (with sections of the challenged peasantries against the excesses of capitalist commodification) or merely moderate (with sections of the rising middle class against aristocratic resistance to the sharing of political power). (Abendroth, 1972)

If there was a consistent rhythm to those early working-class industrial and political struggles, it was this: a rhythm of perennial movement from industrial to political struggle in line with trade cycles and patterns of state repression; and a movement over time from middle-class alliances to peasant/small farmer alliances, as (with aristocratic accommodations to rising middle-class power) many members of the new employing classes lost interest in full democratic political reform. Each national capitalism had its own pattern, of course. It was one fixed largely by the positioning of each economy in the emerging global system, by the resulting space for working-class accommodation each thereby enjoyed, and by the balance of old and new classes consolidated within each. The strength of the peasantry consolidated in the Napoleonic settlements slowed the pace of capitalist industrialization in France throughout the nineteenth century. The absence of any feudal past (and so of intense peasant unrest) freed US elites to grant democratic rights (though not trade union ones) to white male workers prior to full industrialization. The UK period of world dominance created a space for limited trade union recognition and eventually even limited social reform well before 1914; and so on. But in general, the later the industrialization, the harder it was for workers even to establish trade unions without meeting the full repressive powers of the state; and so in general, the later the industrialization the more radical proletarian politics had to be from the very outset. As we will see more fully later, Karl Marx (watching all this unfold in the 1860s and 1870s) thought the revolutionary impulse toward socialism would come from capitalism's core, fueled by its most established working classes; but he was wrong. At the center of world capitalism by 1900 there was just enough economic and political space to allow the consolidation there of moderate working-class politics. It was where that space was entirely missing, in the peripheral capitalisms whose ruling groups were racing to catch up, that the space for the politics of reform was at its weakest, and where revolutionary socialist politics first took a dominant hold.

WORKING-CLASS POLITICS IN EARLY CAPITALISM

From that range of response three broad trajectories emerged which collectively shaped working-class politics in the twentieth century: a trajectory of initial general challenge, a trajectory of isolated revolutionary failure, and a trajectory of ultimate working-class accommodation. (Sassoon, 1996)

There can be no doubt that prior to the 1917–20 period (the years of intense class struggle that accompanied the end of World War I), the battle lines between workers and capitalists in *all* the core economies were drawn around strategies of ruling-class repression and working-class revolutionary challenge. On the Left in all the labor movements of the leading industrial economies, revolutionary socialist voices were a major presence, challenged predominantly only by what would become eventually the more moderate form of working-class politics—namely **social democracy**. That was as true of the US and UK labor movements as it was of the German and the Russian. (G. Adams, 1966; Kendall, 1969; Nettl, 1966) In the end, however, much of that revolutionary talk was exposed as simply posturing, as revolutionary currents were drowned in both the United States and the United Kingdom, and as German Social Democrats split in a fierce internal civil war that saw moderate socialists collaborating with right-wing militias to crush their more revolutionary colleagues. But even so, the 1917–20 period was still one of unprecedented working-class political successes: with the overthrow of autocracies in Central Europe and with the Bolshevik victory in Russia. In consequence, in 1920 the world did literally seem to stand on the threshold of a socialist transformation that would be history's response to the immiserization caused by capitalist industrialization (Mitchell, 1970); and so it made sense to read the Russian Revolution (as both Trotsky and by then Lenin read it) as the spark that would trigger revolutionary upheavals within the core capitalisms, as working classes rallied to the defense of the international proletarian cause by overthrowing their own capitalisms and by assisting Russian workers in the yet-to-be-completed accumulation of capital in Russia itself. (Coates, 2015a: 145–8)

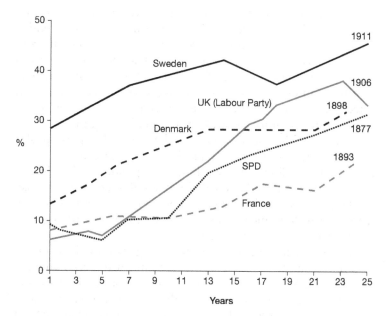

Figure 3.1 Pre-1914 rise of support for socialism in Western Europe

Source: Guttsman (1981: 16)

It did not work out that way of course, and its failure to do so opened two quite distinct trajectories of working-class experience and politics that shaped the rest of the twentieth century. As we first saw in Chapter 1, the ostensibly socialist state called into existence by the Bolshevik Revolution survived in isolated form, and in its isolation degenerated into a party-led regime of terror. As we noted earlier, the Bolshevik Party itself came to play the role historically granted by Marxism to the industrial bourgeoisie: that of developing the forces of production by the rapid proletarianization of originally agrarian labor. The modern Russian working class was first created in the 1930s, in a process of primitive capital accumulation that involved both the forced collectivization of Russian agriculture and the rapid construction of a Russian military-industrial complex and heavy industry manufacturing base. That creation (as earlier in Western

Europe, Japan and the United States) was achieved only by horrendous human suffering: by long hours of labor, intensive work practices, starvation wages, and (in the Russian case) immense terror and ideological control. The socialist project was thereby subverted into one of rapid state/party-led industrialization from an entirely peasant base, and understood in that form acted for a critical generation as a revolutionary model (and a source of revolutionary discipline) for socialists both in the labor movements of the core capitalisms and in certain key pre-capitalist economies to Russia's South and East (not least those of China and Vietnam). Successful working-class politics within Russia were thus blocked; and in the defeat of the Russian working class, by the party ostensibly created to lead and represent it, immense damage was done more generally to the cause of working-class emancipation on a global scale.

Among the key elements of that damage was the increasingly distorting impact of Stalinist conservatism on the revolutionary project within the labor movements of the core capitalisms, and the resulting extra legitimacy given there to more moderate forms of working-class struggle. For the second trajectory emerging from the socialist defeat of 1917–20 was that of social democracy within Western Europe and of militant trade unionism without independent political leadership in the United States. Initially neither the Western European working class nor the North American labor movement was strong enough to impose itself either industrially or politically. Indeed the 1920s and 1930s in Europe were decades of working-class defeat by the forces of the Right: most violently in Italy, Germany and then Spain; more constitutionally in France and the United Kingdom. But American labor emerged from the Depression and the New Deal with an unexpectedly strident and effective industrial militancy and self-confidence (Dray, 2010): a self-confidence which the full mobilization of working-class forces to defeat fascism then spread across Western Europe as a whole. The result of that defeat— differently manifested in both Axis and Allied economies and societies—was a series of class compacts imposed on discredited local employing classes by labor movements radicalized by war.

Employing classes in each core capitalism in turn emerged from World War II faced with the need to accommodate working-class demands for industrial recognition, and for political and social rights, as labor movements emerged—in Germany and Japan no less than in Western Europe and North America—determined that there would be no return to the horrors of the 1930s. In the critical decade that divided the Axis defeat in 1945 from the 1950s **McCarthyite** pushback against both the democratic and the revolutionary Left, militant labor movements (often staffed by returning soldiers hardened by war) then struck a string of easier effort-wage bargains with their local employing classes, so calling into existence over time that new form of capitalism that we first discussed in Chapter 2—*welfare capitalism*—and in the process abandoning entirely any interest in doing anything more to capitalism as a whole than to manage it into a more civilized form.

ENJOYING CAPITALISM'S WELFARE MOMENT

Within the core capitalist economies of Western Europe, North America and Japan, what emerged from the intense class struggles of the immediate post-war decade was a fragile class compromise. It was one built on production regimes within core capitalisms in which the profitability of the largest firms was increasingly a consequence of the systematic application of machinery to production, rather than on the intensification of the labor process. It was built, that is, and as we noted earlier, on Fordism. As we first saw in Chapter 1, the capitalist part of the newly divided world economy then grew without generalized crisis for an entire generation—from 1948 to 1973—but within that economic growth, the new prosperity was highly concentrated in a very restricted group of national capitalisms in Northern Europe, North America and eventually Japan. In those economies, and in those economies alone, the generalized application of machinery to production produced dramatic increases in labor productivity, and eventually allowed a significant rise in both the private and the social wage paid to industrial workers. But in semi-peripheral and peripheral parts of the global system, this rise simply did not occur. Instead, a more limited degree of investment and commodification in those regions produced export sectors in a range of formally/informally colonial territories, and generated a reserve army of mobile labor willing (and indeed often desperate) to migrate to the metropolitan centers of the global system where wages were higher and living conditions better.

So as we saw earlier, for that 25-year period at least the global capitalist production system froze itself into a First World, a Second World and a Third. In the first quarter century following World War II, income inequalities *within* First World economies narrowed as income inequalities *between* First World economies and Second and Third World ones widened. And for that period too, a form of working-class political moderation consolidated itself within the core capitalisms, as issues of rural unrest and the destruction of small-scale manufacturing were pushed out from the core to the periphery, and as the size of the global labor force grew only slowly, and grew only within core capitalist areas. As we have already noted, labor migration was a feature of this immediate post-war period as it had been of the late nineteenth century, but these new labor migrants did not go to create new working classes, or to join working classes that were themselves in the early stages of creation. They went to join labor forces already in existence, to fit into low-paying jobs beneath those occupied by indigenous workers—to act, that is, as reserve armies of labor in a phase of high working-class employment.

Materially and socially, the working and living conditions enjoyed by indigenous workers in this "golden age of capitalism" differed significantly from the proletarian condition of capitalism's first generations.

Materially, the working conditions and living standards of most workers within the core capitalisms began eventually to ease and improve. For a generation after 1945, job security became a reality for the well-organized sections of the industrial labor force in Western Europe, the United States and Japan. In the large industrial and increasingly mechanized plants of the Fordist kind, and in the growing office buildings and public sector bureaucracies with which those plants came progressively to share occupational space, the pace of work eventually slowed; and indeed in some capitalisms (though not in all—the United States was the big exception here) working conditions even came under a degree of informal worker control. And wage levels too rose to well beyond subsistence for the bulk of capitalism's established working classes, as profit-making and successful investment came to depend on the production and sale of wage goods of an increasingly differentiated kind to workers paid adequately enough to afford them, and as welfare bureaucracies proliferated as sources both of employment and of assistance to workers afflicted by unemployment, injury and age. (Coates, 1995: 20–6)

This job security, work control and private and public prosperity was never uniformly distributed within the post-war labor forces of the advanced capitalist economies. It came late (only from the 1960s) in Western Europe. It never extended to non-white, non-male sections of the working class even there; and the social wage in particular was not generalized across even well-organized labor movements in either the United States or Japan. But there was nonetheless a sea change in material experience for large numbers of workers in all the major capitalisms, a sea change when compared to working-class experiences between the wars, and a sea change that rested on the dramatic increase in labor productivity achieved in capitalism's Fordist phase. It was a change which briefly allowed a resetting of capitalism's effort-wage bargain, and it was one which, for many core workers from the mid-1970s, brought levels of personal consumption to new and unanticipated heights. It was not a change, however, which allowed the generalization of this new (and easier) proletarian condition to either industrial or rural workers in non-core capitalisms. There, as in the Soviet bloc, working conditions remained arduous and under-capitalized, labor productivity remained low, and wages and living conditions remained frozen at little above pre-war levels, even as basic labor conditions eased in the heartlands of the global capitalist system.

Socially, the new post-war settlement between capital and labor in the core economies of the global system altered the balance and character of the class forces surrounding industrial production there. The early capitalist world in which displaced rural workers and oppressed factory operatives existed side by side, and in which the employing classes were everywhere small and visible, gave way to one in which rural oppression and factory life became geographically separated: rural struggles becoming increasingly a Third World phenomenon, and factory-based struggles becoming—for a generation at least—almost exclusively a First World monopoly. The early capitalist world also gave way to one in which the growth of large companies and the extension of state roles produced a huge and highly differentiated middle class alongside the hitherto ubiquitous working class. Indeed in the first generations of that new post-World War II middle class, the growth in the number of new supervisory and managerial positions was such that those slots could be filled only by a degree of short-term social mobility from within the working class itself, so helping for a generation (the baby boomer one) slightly to soften and to blur the sharp class divisions of worker and employer that were so striking a feature of the advanced economies' early capitalist period.

Moreover, after 1945 the shortage of labor produced by the class compacts of strong labor movements in the core capitalisms drew new groups into the mainstream of the capitalist employment process. As we just noted, full employment at the core of the system stimulated labor migration, as capitalists looked further and further afield (both geographically and socially) for their reserve army of labor. Full employment at the core also stimulated a post-war migration of labor from countryside to town in capitalisms where the total destruction of the pre-capitalist peasantry had not been completed (in Italy and in Japan in particular). As we saw in Chapter 2, it stimulated the movement of black labor (and later Hispanic labor) north into the US industrial belt. It stimulated the movement of colonial peoples from periphery to core within the European empires (from North Africa to France, from South Asia and the Caribbean to the United Kingdom, from South East Asia to Holland) and it stimulated the movement of workers first from Eastern Europe and then Turkey into a West Germany denied the direct fruits of its brief colonial past. The shortage of labor created by regimes of full employment also stimulated the movement of married women with children back into the paid employment from which they had been increasingly excluded (except in wartime) by the effective closure of manual jobs to women by male-dominated trade unions from the middle of the nineteenth century. (As we will see more clearly in Chapter 5, it was a movement back into paid employment that, from the 1960s, left more and more married women in the core capitalisms with the "double burden" of their own wage work and their unpaid work in the home that reproduced the wage labor of others.) What emerged in consequence was a divided working class in each major national capitalism in turn: a working class divided, at the very least, between a unionized section and a non-unionized section, between private sector workers and public sector ones, between male workers and female workers, and between indigenous workers and labor migrants.

THE RISE AND FALL OF ORGANIZED LABOR

Industrially and politically, these material and social changes gave a new (and more complex) face to the politics of labor. If the dominant industrial and political agenda of early working classes had been the winning of the right to organize and the right to be represented politically, the industrial and political agenda of later generations of similarly placed workers was dominated by the question of how fully to exploit those rights, once won. Their task was to make their voices heard, and to effect real concessions from dominant classes which had now learned to live with independent working-class organization but which were still as reluctant as their predecessors had been to surrender real wealth, control and power. The task for the early working class had been to win the right to sit at the capitalist table. The task of their equivalents post-1945 was to win significant influence over what was to be served there.

The immediate post-war shortage of labor within the industrial circuits of the core capitalist economies—to which we have just referred—generated a small but significant shift in class power. In principle, within the manufacturing factories of each fully employed economy well-organized groups of workers were well-positioned to strike new effort-reward bargains, even slowly to establish a degree of control over aspects of the work process, and to link their wages to rising labor productivity. Politically, those same workers were well-positioned to elect into office parties committed to the maintenance of full employment and the extension of the social wage. In practice, however, the capacity of particular labor movements to strike either of these bargains—the first industrial, the second political—varied in significant ways: with the industrial bargain initially being beyond the reach of labor movements facing capitalist classes defeated in war (so in Germany and Japan); and with the political bargain beyond the reach of working classes which had failed before 1939 to consolidate independent working-class political organizations (critically, in the United States). But across the core capitalisms as a whole, the late 1940s and early 1950s saw the consolidation of class compacts of varying types, compacts which collectively enabled a section of each working class—invariably the male, skilled, unionized sections—to link wages to profitability, and to spread out more equitably the social benefits of the Fordist shift from labor-intensive production systems to semi-automated and technologically sophisticated ones.

While the post-war "golden age of capitalism" lasted—and it lasted for each major industrial capitalism until 1973, and then peeled away progressively for each (starting with the United Kingdom and the United States in the late 1970s and ending with Japan and Germany in the early 1990s)—industrial and political moderation was the order of the day. A generation of workers at the core of the system experienced steadily rising living standards, job security and enhanced welfare provision, and responded accordingly. Among those workers, the predominant industrial response was one focused on the local achievement of better wages and conditions, and the predominant political response was one marking a retreat from more grandiose schemes of system change. The predominant overall response, that is, was a combination of industrial militancy and growing political conservatism. Workers in the core capitalisms pushed for higher wages and easier working conditions, and achieved success in both. They supported parties of the Center-Left, but required of them only a modest resetting of property rights, income distribution and welfare underpinnings. Initially in the post-war period, working-class pressure effected a major resetting of the social architecture of capitalism (with workers pushing for health cover, education and pensions), and at the height of the post-war boom, workers in much of Western Europe struck for a second resetting of the class accord (between 1968 and 1973)—a resetting that called into existence what we would now recognize as a set of fully developed welfare states. But once that new architecture was in place, the pressure of organized workers for its extension weakened and their interest in socialist politics waned.

For by the 1970s the pressure points in the global capitalist system had shifted. They had shifted to movements articulating the grievances of excluded and newly proletarianized workers, movements which often met only ambiguous support (and sometimes even outright resistance) from the organized sections of the male white working class. Within the core capitalisms, radicalism became concentrated in movements of black workers, fleetingly in movements of students opposed to imperial wars, and in the women's movements which sprang briefly to prominence in the 1970s. Beyond the core, radicalism shifted into movements challenging agrarian capitalism, colonial rule and imperial domination—movements that were predominantly peasant-based but within which industrial workers played a significant but subordinate part (marginally in Vietnam, centrally in South Africa). They shifted too (particularly in South America) into a series of peasant-based movements of workers obliged to straddle rural and urban employment while being progressively squeezed in both; and into struggles by newly established industrial workers for basic wages and rights. And between the First World and the Third, working-class pressure was a key ingredient in the sequence of Second World uprisings against Soviet domination: massively so in the East German rebellion of 1953, less dominantly so but still potent in Hungary in 1956 and Czechoslovakia in 1968, and dominant again in Poland from 1980. Throughout it all, however, the voice of the Left was hampered by the persistence of old conservatisms and by the articulation of new ones. Divisions of status, religion and politics split the labor movements of each national capitalism to varying degrees: setting skilled worker against unskilled, Catholic against Protestant, socialist against communist. And ruling-class pressures compounded those divisions. They did so ideologically: initially by the weight of McCarthyite orchestrations of Cold War anti-communism, and later by the renewed challenge of **neo-liberal economics** to the briefly dominant Keynesian consensus. And they did so materially, as employer confidence grew, in a series of offensives against trade union power, against wage increases, and against the taxation necessary for adequate welfare coverage.

Those conservative counterweights to the full development of reformist social compacts could be (and were) held at bay so long as the rhythm of capital accumulation did not falter, and as the associated rise in labor productivity continued to permit wages and profits to rise together. But from 1973 this combination of rising wages and profits was progressively more difficult to effect because labor productivity growth was progressively more difficult to generate—again in a sequence, beginning with the weaker national units in the system (such as the United Kingdom) and ending with even the stronger ones (such as Germany) in internal class tension. The reasons for the unraveling of the post-war class compact were simultaneously economic and political. Economically, even in competitively strong national capitalisms and certainly in the weaker ones, the traditional male-dominated white working class of capitalism's post-1945 "golden age" was increasingly

Table 3.1 The ebb and flow of the UK labor movement

	Trade union membership (000s) & density (%)*		Labour Party: percentage of popular vote at each election	Number of strike days: annual averages (000s)
1945	7,875	42.2	48.3	–
1950	9,289	42.1	46.1	–
1951	9,535	42.9	48.8	–
1955	9,741	42.2	46.4	–
1959	9,623	41.5	43.8	–
1964	10,218	41.6	44.1	–
1966	10,190	41.1	47.9	–
1967	11,179	45.8	43.0	–
1974	11,764	47.4	38.1	1968–1974: 11,703
1979	13,498	53.0	37.0	1975–1979: 11,663
1983	11,337	48.2	27.6	1980–1984: 10,486
1987	10,475	42.8	30.8	1985–1990: 3,600
1992	9,128	36.3	34.4	1991–1996: 656
1997	7,801	29.9	44.4	1997–2001: 357
2001	7,752	26.4	42.0	2002–2006: 728
2005	7,473	24.8	35.2	–
2010	6,500	26.6	29.0	–

Note: * Percentage of the labor force who are union members.

Source: Taylor (1993), Daniels & McIlroy (2009) and Achur (2011)

undermined from the 1970s by processes of **deindustrialization** that moved more and more employment out of heavy manual work and manufacturing into ever growing service sectors characterized by low labor productivity, low wages and low levels of trade union organization. And politically the response of employing classes everywhere to the growing difficulty of combining rising profits and rising wages as the rate of labor productivity slowed from the 1970s was ultimately the same: the retreat of capital from industrial circuits to financial ones; the export of remaining industrial capital to easier labor markets; and the internal resetting of class compacts, this time *against* labor rather than in its favor.

In these new conditions of intensified employer offensives and capital flight, the weakening of the degree of working-class industrial and political solidarity achieved during capitalism's brief "golden age" left established labor movements vulnerable to the incremental deconstruction of the gains each had made. The last quarter of the twentieth century therefore saw a systematic rolling back of the political and industrial power of organized labor, without however triggering a generalized shift to the Left among workers now subject again to an intensification of the labor process, stagnant/falling real wages and enhanced job insecurity (of a kind more generally associated with capitalism's early stages). Strong labor unions, full employment and expanding welfare services were key to the first post-war growth period experienced by the core capitalist economies between 1948 and 1973. Deliberately weakened unions and welfare retrenchment became a key feature of the second growth period between 1992 and 2008; and did so—in economies such as those of the United States and the United Kingdom—*before* the large-scale entry of Chinese exports into global markets in the first decade of the new millennium then helped to pull wage levels in core capitalisms down further still.

Increasingly disillusioned with conventional politics as general living standards stagnated and working conditions deteriorated during that second growth period, male white workers within the core capitalisms proved disproportionately vulnerable on either side of the new millennium to right-wing ideas and political projects. At worst, they retreated into new cultures of privatized entertainment, alcohol and sport, and re-invigorated old cultures of patriarchy, nationalism and racism. At best, they retained an affection for social democratic welfare institutions and a belief in the need to retain them by re-electing governments of the Center-Left, but this time without any great faith in the ability of their political leaders to actually deliver much in the way of economic and social reform. Residual pockets of more generalized militancy remained—politically in the French labor movement, industrially in the German and for a time the American—but by the end of the century the heroic days of working-class struggle were, for most established working classes in core capitalisms, a distant memory. By then, the center of labor struggles had shifted out from the core of the global system: breaking the mold of Soviet power in political revolutions at the end of the 1980s; and challenging the dominance of industrial classes in the new capitalisms (in East Asia) and peripheral capitalisms (in South America) to which so much of the mobile industrial investment funds of more established capitalist classes were by then gravitating. It was not that, as the new millennium dawned, capitalism's basic class struggle was over. It was much more a matter of the game being simply paused at half-time, with the center of action shifting out of the conceptual "North" and heading "East" and "South."

OLD AND NEW CAPITALISMS LIVING TOGETHER

For by the first decades of the twenty-first century, the global balance of class forces was again in flux—a flux characterized this time (as we mentioned at the start of this chapter) by a complex layering of old working classes and new, and by a complex interweaving of profit and investment rhythms based on the intensification of the labor process with profit and investment rhythms based on the deployment of modern technologies.

The export of capital had by then created (and is still now continuing to create) whole new working classes, in renewed processes of primitive capital accumulation which—as we noted earlier—are prizing vast numbers of peasants out of the Asian (and on a smaller scale, the South American and southern African) countryside. As recently as 1980, the total workforce in the capitalist part of the global system (in the core capitalisms, parts of Africa and most of South America) numbered just less than 1 billion people. But by the year 2000, population growth within that area (but mainly outside the core capitalisms) had already taken that number to 1.46 billion; and the additional 1.47 billion "workers from China, India and the former Soviet bloc [who also] entered the global labor pool" in the 1980s and 1990s then "*doubled* the size of the world's now-connected workforce" (Freeman, 2010) as the new millennium began. That huge 2.93 billion number had crept up to 3.15 billion by 2013, if the International Labor Organization (ILO) calculations are right, so effectively *tripling* the number of workers competing in capitalist labor markets in the three and a half decades since the election of Reagan and Thatcher.

In the emerging capitalist economies of South and South East Asia, in parts of the Middle East, in parts of southern Africa and Latin America, and even in the pseudo-socialist economy of China, economies that were once predominantly peasant-based (with small mining and industrial enclaves) are now (and have been for more than three decades) transforming themselves into wage labor-based economies, with large (though still minority) industrial working classes and extensive rural proletariats, and even larger informal sectors in which marginal workers eke out a meager subsistence through complex and fluid mixtures of wage work, petty trade and subsistence agriculture. In many of these new economies, that informal sector is often extremely large: in South Africa, for example, currently sustaining perhaps one worker in every three. (Wills, 2009) And alongside them, already more heavily industrialized economies such as Brazil, Argentina and Mexico have continued to maintain (or even increase) the proportion of their labor forces employed in the industrial sector, putting them now at levels—around 25 percent—that are matched in advanced capitalisms only by economies such as Germany and Japan. (World Bank, 2014)

Many of those caught up in this second great wave of primitive capital accumulation moved directly into factories that were themselves equipped with modern sophisticated machinery, and proved capable of quickly establishing there recognizably distinct working-class institutions and militancy; but many did not. For even in the economies that have now been industrializing on a large scale for more than three decades, many of their new industrial workers met fierce state repression and resistance whenever they sought to organize and press for better wages/working conditions, particularly in authoritarian regimes free of any constitutional or democratic impediments to political violence. China today, Brazil under the generals, South Korea for most of the post-war period are clear examples of regimes blocking independent working-class organization, and of labor forces subject to control in part through state-sponsored trade unions of the kind long established in the Soviet Union. (Short, 2014) And still more of these new workers were not industrially concentrated and capital equipped in this fashion. They still worked (and still do to this day) with primitive technologies, obliged to trade subsistence (or less than subsistence) wages for long hours and primitive and intense working conditions, and to do so to meet the profit requirements of large transnational corporations just as much as those of local small-scale employers. (Citizens Trade Campaign, 2014)

Moreover, this is the modern proletarian condition not just in the new mines and sweatshops of South and East Asia. It is also the proletarian condition of growing numbers of workers within the advanced capitalisms themselves, as a growing subproletariat emerges there of building workers, agricultural laborers and service employees closed off by ethnicity, language and trade union impotence from the established labor movement around them. In an economy such as the one surrounding me as I draft this—in North Carolina—people living in the same town can be (and indeed often are) operating in entirely different global labor markets: some competing with workers working in similar industries in places such as Bangladesh (so effectively operating in what once might have been labeled a Third World labor market) while others remain remarkably free of any significant competition outside of the United States itself. By the year 2000 a whole new international division of labor had blown away the old distinctions between First World, Second and Third, and between North, South and East. By 2000 the North had gone South (in the form of extensive Asian, southern African and South American industrialization). The South had come North (in the form particularly of the increasing number of South American workers in the North American working class); and the East had come West, with the collapse of Soviet Communism and the re-entry of an Eastern European/Russian set of established labor forces into the circuits of global accumulation.

In consequence old and new working classes now co-habit the capitalist world as never before, bringing together workers battling to cope with newly established capitalist classes and workers battling to cope with long-established ones. The experience and agendas of primitive capital accumulation are now being lived again worldwide. Even the World Bank conceded as much: noting that as recently as 1995, "the more than a billion individuals [then] living on a dollar or less a day depend[ed] . . . on pitifully low returns to hard work. In many countries workers lack[ed] representation, and work[ed] in unhealthy, dangerous or demeaning conditions." (cited in Harvey, 1998: 64–5) And even now, as the ILO reported in June 2014, "839 million workers in developing countries are unable to earn enough to lift themselves and their families above the US$2 a day poverty threshold. This represents around one-third of total employment, compared with over half in the early 2000's." (ILO, 2014: xx)

Older and more established working classes too now have a new agenda. It is at least one now freed of a distorted Marxism in the former Soviet Union. It is one of an eroding welfare capitalism in much of Western Europe. It is one of intensified work routines and long working hours even in the United States itself. There is very little space, in this new global capitalism, for any particular working class to hide or to benefit from special privileges. Everywhere the working-class story is one of the ratcheting down of established wages and conditions where won, and the denial of adequate wages and standards where not. There is a venality to contemporary capitalism that was always obvious to workers in its under-developed sections, a venality partially hidden for half a century from well-organized workers in its central core. We are nearer now to the capitalism of *The Communist Manifesto* than we have ever been: a capitalism so single-minded in its pursuit of profits that all of its working classes are, as Marx and Engels argued long ago, "at last compelled to face with sober senses [their] real conditions of life, and [their] relations with their kind." (Marx & Engels, 1848: 38)

In a very crucial sense, this co-habitation of old and new working classes offers both a fresh set of possibilities and a fresh set of dilemmas for anyone keen to create a prosperous and equitable future for the entirety of humankind. It offers a fresh set of possibilities because the arrival of new working classes necessarily rekindles radical agendas increasingly abandoned by more established labor movements; and it creates a fresh set of dilemmas because the articulation of old and new labor forces in a shared global space makes the linking of working-class struggles both a pressing and yet a uniquely complex task. The forces striving to divide workers find much on which to build in this new conjuncture: issues of scale, legacies of history, the revival of reactionary religions, and the strength and avarice of ruling classes all combine to set workers apart even more than before. But more progressive forces are not without their structural and social underpinnings too: not least in the linkage of workers through the emergence of **commodity chains**, the rise of transnational corporations, the increased export of capital and commodities, the shared experience of world economic government by the **WTO**, and the generalized assault made by local employers and states on whatever level of working-class remuneration and job control has thus far been achieved. As we noted at the start of this chapter, how far this clash of alternative forces— good and bad, progressive or reactionary—will create a more or a less humane form of capitalism going forward remains the open question of the age. It is a question to which of necessity, therefore, we will return in the closing pages of this volume.

FOR FURTHER EXPLORATION

On the history of working-class struggles, begin with Thompson (1963) and go to Sassoon (1996). On working conditions and the labor experience, start with Braverman (1974) and go to Beiler et al. (2008), Perelman (2011), Huws (2014) and Atzeni (2014).

4

CAPITALISM IN CONTENTION

For reasons that presumably now are fairly obvious, given the enormous impact of capitalism on the way we live, people have been debating its nature from its inception. Indeed there is an important sense in which disagreements about the character and consequence of organizing economic life on capitalist lines actually triggered the nineteenth-century emergence of what we would now recognize as modern social science. Moreover, such disagreements certainly stood at the heart of the twentieth-century debate on how best to organize advanced industrial societies; and in this new century they remain key elements dividing electorates (and their attendant intellectuals) in advanced capitalist societies, in former communist societies, and across the under-developed world. If we are to make sense of contemporary capitalism and its potential futures, therefore, we too need to pick our way through at least the best of the various intellectual traditions that have emerged as capitalism has developed. That mapping will not solve the choices of thought that we each need to make; but it will, if done properly, help significantly to clarify the nature of the choices themselves.

PARADIGMS OF EXPLANATION

The question is how to do that mapping simply and effectively. It is not necessarily easy. After all, there is a huge amount of relevant literature out there. My own view, developed over several decades of struggling with this issue, is that it is worth likening the act of understanding capitalism to that of standing on a stage—a stage that is illuminated, from the rafters far above, by shafts of light beamed down upon it by powerful spotlights, each one of which illuminates part of the stage by leaving the rest in full or semi-darkness. For our purposes, each of those spotlights should be thought of as a major intellectual tradition— one that has been widened over time by the writings of later adherents, but one that was initially anchored in the bright lights (the writings) of just a few key individuals. To my mind, there are at least three such broad intellectual traditions worthy of our consideration. One stretches back to the writings of Adam Smith and through him to the philosophical ruminations of John Locke. A second stretches back to the writings of Karl Marx, and through him to Georg Wilhelm Friedrich Hegel; and there is a third, more complex and less coherent, intellectual tradition worthy of note whose founding "fathers" include at least Max Weber in Germany (and stretching back through him, Immanuel Kant) and in England John Maynard Keynes (and through him, John Stuart Mill). If we are to understand where we have come from as contemporary members of societies shaped by centuries of capitalism, if we are to understand what is happening to that capitalism now, and if we are to gain at least some purchase on what possibly looms before us, we need at the very least to familiarize ourselves with the three intellectual traditions labeled here as "classical liberalism," "Marxism" and "social reformism."

But before we close in on the detail of how those intellectual traditions differ in their specification of capitalism and its dynamics, we need to note several features that they hold in common. One is that each is best thought of as a distinct *paradigm*, using that term as a way of understanding intellectual development within the social sciences in much the same manner that Thomas Kuhn once used it to explain intellectual developments in the natural sciences. (Kuhn, 1962) Thomas Kuhn documented the way in

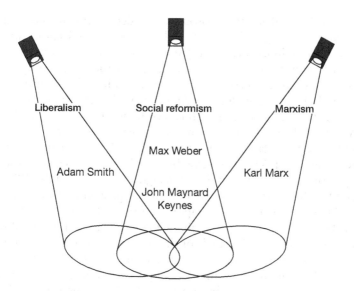

Figure 4.1 Paradigms as searchlights in the social sciences

which dominant ways of understanding the natural world changed dramatically over time. He showed how a long-established set of medieval assumptions rooted in Catholic theology and Aristotelian categories of analysis was initially swept away by the writings of scientists such as Copernicus, Galileo and Newton, only for their dominant ways of thought to be challenged centuries later by the writings of Albert Einstein. In Kuhn's world of the natural sciences, as in ours of the social sciences, it made sense to think of major intellectual traditions as being distinct paradigms: that is, it made sense to think of each having its own *ontology* and *epistemology* (its own view of the human condition and of the kinds of knowledge of that condition that are open to the individuals participating in it), its own *core categories of analysis* and associated *explanations*, and its own agreed *methodologies* and set of main *texts*. In the natural sciences, Kuhn tells us, one set of dominant understandings tended entirely to replace another over time, as the problems which the original paradigm could not address were adequately handled by the paradigm that eventually (and for that reason) superseded it. But in the social sciences, paradigms have not, and do not, rise and fall in quite that fashion. Individual paradigms do have periods of dominance. Social reformism was the conventional wisdom of the age in advanced capitalist economies in the generation after World War II; and classical liberalism made a powerful reappearance in the thought of the generation influenced by Ronald Reagan and by Margaret Thatcher. But even social science paradigms that are suddenly out of favor never entirely vanish. Market liberals, social reformers and Marxists have been debating capitalism—each operating in their own distinct paradigm—since at least the 1850s; and the debate is, even now, showing no propensity to go away.

There are at least two important reasons for the persistence of these core disagreements about the character and potential of capitalism. One is that each of the intellectual paradigms still in play in the on-going debate about capitalism is actually *very good*. Each does illuminate important aspects of our contemporary condition. Each does light up part of the stage. The other is that each of these intellectual frameworks has now been around long enough, and has had enough explanatory capacity to win itself new converts as one generation replaces another, to have become an important *part* of the capitalist world that its categories of analysis help us to understand. In that sense, each of these three intellectual traditions now has a distinct presence on the very stage which it—and its competitor traditions—is struggling to illuminate. For the three paradigms we will examine here are more than simply *intellectual traditions* (though they are certainly that, and as such available to us as storehouses of ideas, categories and approaches). They are also *political ideologies*, bodies of ideas associated with particular political parties and social movements; and they also have a capacity to exist at the level of popular consciousness. For to the degree that those political parties or movements manage over a long period to spread their ideologies so wide and deep in society that people momentarily lose their ability to see that they are subscribing to a coherent and particular body of thought at all, each of our three intellectual traditions has the capacity to become literally the *common sense* of their age. In different countries and at different times, each of the three intellectual traditions that we will now examine have been briefly hegemonic in that fashion; and even when that hegemony has been lost, strong residues of each tradition remain present in the dominant discourses of the day.

So even now, the adherents of classical liberalism of the kind associated with the later writings of Adam Smith are real players in the modern policy debate, doing their level best to create a world in their understanding of Smith's image. Likewise, adherents of the case for a managed and reformed capitalism first developed by late Victorian "new liberals" (and later given a distinctly twentieth-century economic presence by John Maynard Keynes) are still battling classical liberalism for ideological and political dominance. Marxism is less of a presence in the current debate: at least, it is less of a presence in the intellectual repertoires of most leading universities in the English-speaking world than it was a generation ago. For the distortion of its message in the degeneration of the Russian Revolution threw a long shadow over Marxism as a source for understanding capitalism, challenging its legitimacy and appropriateness; but as that shadow now steadily fades, its adherents too have a powerful voice to bring back to the table. Classical liberals tell us now, and have been telling us since at least the publication of Adam Smith's *The Wealth of Nations* in 1776, that we would do well to understand the world that capitalism has created as simply comprising self-interested individuals who are perfectly capable of rationally pursuing their own private goals, and as such are best left to themselves—free from all but the minimum of government regulation. Social reformers, by contrast, have long told us—and tell us now—that although the world created by modern capitalism is complex and inter-connected, those inter-connections work best when open to incremental reform and democratic management. And Marxists, less optimistic than both, continue to insist that the world created by capitalism is inevitably dominated by the contradictions of interests of the classes that make it up, such that a capitalism which is unregulated is unstable, and a capitalism which is regulated is but a stage *en route* to its eventual total replacement.

All three intellectual traditions cannot be fully correct, of course. Capitalism cannot simultaneously be perfect, imperfect or doomed. But one of these intellectual traditions may well be essentially right. One of them may well be a fully accurate guide to capitalism's past, present and future. Certainly each of them—both independently and in dialogue with the others—draws attention to dimensions of our modern condition on which every one of us needs to hold both an informed opinion and an associated propensity to act. Which is why there is great value in examining the nature and dynamics of capitalism through the lens of first one of these intellectual traditions, and then a second and eventually a third. So first, back to Adam Smith.

CAPITALISM THROUGH THE LENS OF CLASSICAL LIBERALISM

The initial reaction of emerging economic science in eighteenth-century Britain to the arrival of large-scale trade and (eventually) industry was broadly positive. As merchants consolidated their social power and the English landowning classes became heavily involved in commercialized agriculture, liberal ideas flourished. In opposition to arguments about the divine rights of kings and the special privileges of those with inherited wealth, liberal thinkers argued for the rights of the individual—if initially only for the rights of the white male version of the species. They constructed a view of the world as one composed of independent and rational-thinking actors, each equipped with a set of inalienable rights. They recognized the propensity of such a world to quickly become anarchic and brutal without a set of basic rules to constrain excessive behavior, so they argued too for the creation of a state whose sole purpose was to protect the life, liberty and property of all. From this emerging liberal perspective, a government doing more than that would slide back toward tyranny again; and in this way liberalism was born with both a need for, and a deep-seated suspicion of, the activity of the state.

Adam Smith's analysis of the economics of this emerging society was fully in this tradition. Smith's world was made up of people making and selling things, and of people driven to do so only through their own ambition for personal success. For Adam Smith, this was all to the good. It was to be encouraged. The only question was how all these personal ambitions were to be coordinated and, more to the point, how they were to be coordinated in a way that would bring the maximum benefit to all.

Pre-liberal thought and practice would have given that task to the church or the state. But for Adam Smith, neither was necessary and indeed each would only make matters worse. For he believed that the free and undisturbed play of market forces could act as the great unseen hand, efficiently and effectively coordinating the activities of free individuals in ways that advanced the interests of all. As he put it of the emerging capitalist entrepreneur:

> he is, in this as in so many other cases, led by an invisible hand to promote an end which was no part of his intention. Nor is it always the worse for the society that it was not part of it. By pursuing his own interest he frequently promotes that of society more effectively than when he really intends to promote it.
>
> (Smith, 1776: Book 4, Chapter 2, 354)

It was the interplay of supply and demand, the uninterrupted movement of prices and goods, which would—in Smith's view—ultimately enhance the wealth of nations and underpin the freedom of the new producing and consuming individuals within them. All that was left for the state to do was to hold the ring: to provide external defense and internal order, and to supplement private endeavors with certain public institutions that private profit alone could not sustain (the main example of which, for Adam Smith, was publicly funded education). To do more would be to *interfere* (and indeed this notion of state "interference" shows just how strongly classical liberal thought was prepared to privilege the individual and the private over the collective and the public). A "free market" and a "strong but restrained state" became liberalism's vision of an ideal economic and political world.

This classically liberal view of market forces also gave liberal political economists a way of explaining world trade. According to David Ricardo, writing a generation after Adam Smith, economies should specialize under the logic of market competition in the production of those commodities for whose creation they were best equipped—in the production of those things in which they had a comparative advantage. By specializing in this way, they would both enhance the productivity of their own economy and further the growth of wealth in the world economy as a whole. If the liberal view was right, whole economies, like the individuals within them, best guaranteed the interests of everyone by simply looking after themselves: free and unregulated competition between nations, just like free and unregulated competition between individuals, was the key to prosperity for all.

Smith and Ricardo were formative figures in an entire school of liberal political economy which came to public prominence, first in the United Kingdom and then in the United States, in the decades after 1800. Nineteenth-century liberal economists saw a new world of trade and industry emerging, and were conscious of its immense potentiality. By 1820 at the latest, their moral vision of an ideal liberal universe was in place. In an ideal liberal world, individuals would be free—free from political constraints, free from monopolies, free to act alone, free to produce independently and to trade without barriers, and free to enhance the common good by the unbridled pursuit of their own self-interest. By the 1820s, the notions of individual freedom and capitalist enterprise had been fused into a liberal vision that reinforced the confidence of a rising industrial and commercial class. It was a vision, moreover, which rose to public prominence as that class rose to political power. As Keynes later said, "Ricardo's doctrine conquered England as completely as the Holy Inquisition conquered Spain" (Keynes, 1936: 32); so that by the third quarter of the nineteenth century the tradition we have just examined was to all intents and purposes the "conventional wisdom" of the age.

This classical liberal view of the world has a powerful optimism written into it, which has long been part of its appeal. It is an optimism about the rationality of individuals and in their basic ability to benefit everyone by simply getting on with their own lives; an optimism that history is the story of wealth creation and cultural progress if people are only left free to do their own thing; and an overwhelming optimism that markets are the great clearers and coordinators of economic life. This optimism about markets was tempered in Adam Smith's case by his awareness that progress could be derailed by human frailty—he was a professor of moral philosophy, after all (Otteson, 2011)—but as is so often the way with formative thinkers, those who followed him were less sophisticated in their understandings of the human condition.

Optimism about markets was their great legacy to classical liberal thought (and to the neo-classical economic thought that followed it), and with it came a specification of the new "evil." For since markets operate through the competition of individuals within them, what became undesirable was anything which interfered with the ability of competitive markets to function fully. That evil, of course, was monopoly: political monopoly (in the form of an interventionist and regulatory state); labor monopoly (in the form of strong trade unions); and even commercial monopoly (in the form of big firms able to set prices in the marketplace).

This view of markets has never since gone away. It has periodically been "drowned" in public discussion of economics by more interventionist and radical views; but it has never entirely vanished. In fact, it has tended to enjoy intellectual and political domination whenever markets have been doing well (that is, in periods of growth and prosperity) or whenever government intervention has failed to generate that growth. Faith in markets was particularly strong in the Victorian period of industrial supremacy, as Keynes noted; and that faith returned on a grand scale in both the United Kingdom and United States in the decades that followed the stagflation of the 1970s—a stagflation that ended the post-war growth period based on Keynes' own writings. Indeed the potency of the 1980s' turn in public policy back toward **monetarism**, privatization and market deregulation—and the associated rediscovery of the writings not just of Smith but of later liberals such as **Friedrich Hayek** and **Milton Friedman**—is an important indication of what is undoubtedly a more general truth here. Namely that this classical brand of liberalism needs to be understood not simply as one of the earliest and most coherent responses to the rise of capitalism, but also as one of the most all-pervasive, influential and tenacious of all the responses that were to come later.

CAPITALISM THROUGH THE LENS OF MARXISM

Karl Marx, who spent the first two decades of his adult life in Germany watching the rise and fall of middle-class political protest and his last three and a half decades in London observing the consolidation of UK industrial dominance, developed a very different view of capitalism and its potential to the classical liberal one we have just described. Fully conversant with the writings of Smith and Ricardo, he agreed with them that market processes were now central to economic life; feudalism had indeed given way to capitalism. But this did not mean that the social classes of feudal Europe had somehow miraculously dissolved into the classless individuals of their liberal vision. On the contrary, for Marx, the dominant social transformation associated with the rise of capitalism was not one of class dissolution. It was rather one of class replacement: the dislodging of the old classes of feudal Europe (largely aristocracies and peasantries) by the new classes of capitalist Europe (**bourgeoisies** and **proletariats**). The individualism of which Adam Smith spoke, and the liberal political theory from which he drew inspiration, were for Marx merely the dominant form which the ideas of this rising bourgeoisie took to explain their interests and their power.

Where Adam Smith saw a "free exchange between equals" in the market place, Karl Marx saw the playing out of class privilege. He stressed that beneath what he called "the noisy sphere of exchange" (Marx, 1867: Chapter 4, 164) labor was also being bought and sold; and in the social relationships of capitalism's labor markets, class inequalities remained firmly entrenched. Market processes were therefore less the key to human happiness, as classical liberalism would have it, more a key economic mechanism through which the capitalist class realized its profits. For the processes of exchange (in the market) on which classical liberals would have us concentrate were only part of the full circuit of capital. Production was part of that capital too, and there class struggle persisted and indeed—Marx thought—would likely intensify. Far from guaranteeing the mutual needs of all, market processes under capitalism—according to Marx—were both anarchic and destabilizing; and indeed, through the crises of over-production which they inevitably generated, capitalist-directed market processes would eventually inspire the working class to adopt socialism and thereby bring capitalism down.

Marx's attitude to capitalism was therefore quite different from that of Smith and Ricardo. It was not, however, an entirely negative attitude. On the contrary, Marx realized that the emergence of a class of capitalists competing with each other had developed (and was still developing) the productive forces of the economy as a whole, and doing so in ways that the class relationships dominant in feudalism had never been able to do. Competition was the great locomotive of economic growth under capitalism, as Smith had recognized; and to this degree at least, Marx and Smith were in full agreement. History was indeed the story of progress. Classical liberalism and Marxism both possess this underlying optimism about progress over time. It was just that, for Marx, the route to that progress was far stormier and more contradictory than liberalism allowed; and for him at least, that history did not end with capitalism. Capitalism for him was simply one mode of production in a sequence of modes of production; and all modes of production, for Marx, in the end had to succumb to the internal contradictions of class interests around which it was built. Production in classical antiquity in the end succumbed to the limits of a slave-based mode of production, just as later feudalism succumbed to the limits of a serf-based mode. Capitalism would ultimately falter too.

Capitalism's historic role, for Marx, was to create the economic conditions for a society of abundance. Once this had been created, in the hothouse of capitalist inequalities, more egalitarian and less exploitative sets of social relationships—to wit, socialism—would become possible for the first time; and when that time arose, capitalism's job would be done. As Marx put it in 1857, in the dying days of any particular mode of production a moment arrives at which "from forms of development of the productive forces, these social relations turn into their fetters. At that point an era of social revolution begins." (Marx, 1857: 182) Smith had capitalism going on forever. Marx, by contrast, saw capitalism as simply a stage in a longer story that would move humankind from the brutalities and deprivations of classical antiquity through feudalism and capitalism and on to the abundance and ease of socialism and communism.

It was Marx's view—writing in the middle of the nineteenth century—that the industrial capitalism now emerging around him had already largely completed its historic mission, and so needed to be replaced. Later Marxists were even more convinced that this was so, and in the class struggles of the years up to and immediately after World War I saw an epoch of social revolution brought into being by the inherent contradictions of an economically dynamic but socially divided capitalism. Indeed, the sharpest point of contrast between liberal and Marxist readings of the new market-based industrial economies lay here, in their differing attitudes to the economies' stability and long-term capacity to survive in a capitalist form. Liberal thought emphasized the market's capacity to harmonize interests for the benefit of all. Marx emphasized instead the anarchy and crisis-ridden nature of market forces in economies organized on capitalist lines. It was his view that economic crises were endemic to capitalism, and that they would intensify over time. They were endemic because ultimately capitalism will be unable to pay its workers enough to buy all the goods which their labor produced: such that all the future could hold was the increasing immiserization of the proletariat and its associated crises of *under-consumptionism* (or over-production). Crises were also thought by Marx to be endemic to capitalism because anarchic competition between capitalists inevitably put one sector of production, and then another sector, out of proportion with the rest, in the process generating what he termed crises of *disproportionality*. And crises would get worse, he thought, because capitalist production relied on the generation of profits solely from the labor of the proletariat, and that *rate of profit would inevitably fall* as machinery replaced human labor in the productive systems of ever larger capitalist units. Crises of over-production, crises of disproportionality, and a tendency of the rate of profit to fall—Marx's capitalism was not at all as stable and benign as that of Smith and Ricardo!

Marx was not arguing here that capitalism would inevitably be replaced by socialism as crises intensified and profits fell: only that capitalism, through the social dislocations that its economic crises inevitably generated, would ultimately create the social force—the revolutionary working class—that could sweep it away. Marx expected class relationships in capitalist-based societies to simplify and polarize over time, as more and more small-scale producers were reduced to the status of wage laborers (as their businesses were overwhelmed by competition from larger firms), and as the ferocity of competition between the remaining firms made the intensification of labor processes and periodic bouts of mass unemployment unavoidable for the workers they employed.

It is true that (in the years between his death in 1883 and the outbreak of war in 1914) later Marxists recognized, as Marx himself had not, that the contradictions of capital and labor at the core of the emerging global system could be ameliorated for a while by exploiting still more intensely the labor of peasantries and emerging proletariats in less developed capitalisms—that the central contradictions of capitalism could be pushed out for a while from the core to the periphery of the global system. They recognized, that is, that capitalism might pass through a phase of imperialism before succumbing to its final demise. But ultimately it would succumb. Both they and Marx remained convinced that eventually, as more and more people found themselves working together in adverse conditions in bigger and bigger employment units, capitalism would call into existence a proletariat committed to the replacement of capitalism by socialism. On a bad day, Marx was prepared to concede that this radicalization of workers would still be a problematic process, requiring astute political leadership. But on good days, his confidence in the impending fall of capitalism was quite overwhelming—and to later socialists, highly infectious. As he put it in *The Communist Manifesto*, "what the bourgeoisie thereby produces, above all, is its own gravediggers. Its fall and the victory of the proletariat are equally inevitable." (Marx & Engels, 1848: 46)

CAPITALISM AND SOCIAL REFORM

Karl Marx was and remains a highly controversial figure in the history of both capitalism and its analysis, but he shared at least one other characteristic with more mainstream analysts such as Adam Smith. He, like Smith, was committed to a holistic understanding of capitalism—writing in an inter-related way about its economics, its politics, its sociology *and* its philosophy. He was, in that sense, one of the last great holistic thinkers of the Victorian period, one whose type of work was replaced in centrality later by more specialized kinds of writing and more focused forms of social science scholarship. As we will see in more detail in the next chapter, Marx had a lot to say about the class divisions and social structure of the industrial capitalism emerging around him. So too, a generation later, did the great German sociologist **Max Weber**. Marx had even more to say about the economic drivers and sources of crisis in the unregulated capitalism he so disliked. So too, two generations later, did John Maynard Keynes. But there is no distinct economic theory associated with Weber, and no political sociology associated with Keynes. As the twentieth century dawned, we move into different and more fragmented scholarship on the character of capitalism.

Social reformism as portrayed here is very much closer as an intellectual tradition to classical liberalism than it is to Marxism. In fact if we had more space in which to pursue the writings of John Stuart Mill, Max Weber and John Maynard Keynes in more detail, we would probably come to see them—as they certainly came to see themselves—as *troubled* liberals, but as liberals nonetheless. As analysts of capitalism, Mill, Weber and Keynes all shared with classical liberalism a set of assumptions about the importance of the individual, the key role of markets, and the relationship of freedom to the rule of law. But what many twentieth-century social reformers increasingly came to lack was the huge confidence displayed by early liberals in the potential of untrammeled market forces and unbridled self-interest to automatically generate a stable and just social order. Instead, and in this center intellectual ground, we find a growing awareness that although markets do work well as allocators of economic resources they do not work perfectly, and that because they do not, if uncontrolled they are likely to generate undesirable social consequences. In this center ground too, we find an increasing awareness over time of the way in which circumstances change people as well as people change circumstances, such that if people are to enjoy the individual freedoms that liberals cherish, public intervention will be periodically necessary to recreate a level playing field on which people can be equally free—if only to off-set the tendency of unregulated capitalism to create income and wealth inequalities that, if unchallenged, persist and deepen from one generation to the next.

So by the end of the nineteenth century, when a discernible social reformist current first became evident in contemporary debates on social issues, many intellectuals within that current would often still call themselves liberals—but this time **new liberals**, precisely to differentiate themselves from the unreconstructed advocates of *laissez-faire* with whom they were by then in such sharp political disagreement. These new liberals looked to the state, as earlier liberals had not, to guarantee not simply a set of **negative freedoms**—freedoms from state-levied constraints on the individual ability to act—but also a set of more **positive freedoms**—the provision of the resources necessary for people to be able to act independently at all. The pursuit of positive freedoms turned many of these new liberals into powerful advocates of genuine civil rights, into proponents of extensive systems of publicly provided mass education and, in certain cases at least, into campaigners for the democratic management of private economic activity. A classically liberal-based caution about the dangers of too much state activity is still evident in much of their writings, particularly in those of Max Weber (on whom, more later). But by the 1930s at least, that fear of a too-active and too-interventionist state had given way in priority in many social reformist circles to a greater fear. It had given way to the fear that, if unregulated, capitalism would indeed create the revolutionary working class that would, as Marx had predicted, sweep away in their entirety both capitalist property relationships and middle-class political power. The importance of the publication in 1936 of John Maynard Keynes' *General Theory of Employment, Interest and Money* cannot be overstated when that fear is recognized, for what Keynes did in that volume was to provide an economic theory to sustain the middle ground in capitalist politics—a middle ground that could save capitalism from itself, by regulating it away from its anarchic tendencies and moving it toward a dynamism that was stable instead.

By the mid-1930s, Keynes was already a well-established critic of what he termed "unregulated capitalism" and "orthodox economic theory." In direct opposition to that orthodoxy, he argued that the unemployment of the 1930s could not be solved by cutting government spending and money wages, as leading policy-makers in the UK Treasury appeared to think. Of course he was aware that cutting wages would enable employers to lower their prices, as his critics emphasized. But he realized that cutting wages had two effects, not one. It enabled employers to reduce their prices, retain more of their income as profits, and hopefully sell more of their now cheaper goods. But at the same time it reduced the purchasing power of the workers whose wages were cut, and left business confidence low, with employers able to sell less. Keynes became increasingly aware through the 1930s of what we would now recognize as capitalism's central fallacy of composition: that action that was rational for one individual employer (like cutting wages) was not necessarily rational for all employers taken together. In fact Keynes was not convinced that cutting money wages would actually reduce the real purchasing power of workers, since prices would also fall, to leave the real wage situation unaltered but the real value of company debts and taxation much increased. But he was convinced that it was better to tackle the Depression by expanding the economy and allowing prices to rise; since this too would not only reduce real wages (so long as money wages remained unaltered) but would also ease the burden of corporate debt, so boosting business confidence and investment levels.

Against the argument of generalized wage-cutting, therefore, Keynes insisted that if full employment was to be achieved, it would come only as a consequence of firms somehow being able to produce and sell goods again in large quantities and so employ more people. In the conditions of the 1930s, he argued that what a healthy capitalism required was more demand and more spending, not less demand and more saving: that the generation of large-scale employment again could be best triggered by redistributing income from the high savers (the rich) to the low savers (the poor), and by the government spending more money itself. In the absence of private sector confidence in the immediate economic future, the government could generate a multiplier effect through the whole economy—so eroding this lack of private sector confidence—by an expansion of its own labor force, by its own investment spending, and by its purchase of the products of the private sector. It was Keynes' more general view that individuals pursuing their own self-interest in unregulated capitalist markets would not necessarily produce an outcome that was harmonious and advantageous to all. For markets depend for their effective working on *expectations*. In particular, amid the world of uncertainties inherent to capitalist markets, they depend for their working on the employer's expectation of his/her ability to make a profit. If that expectation was not there, an employer would engage fewer workers. With fewer workers employed, the wage incomes available to buy goods would be less; and in this way a downward spiral of unemployment, low wages and more unemployment would inevitably follow. For Keynes, there was no "invisible hand" operating inside unregulated capitalist markets to produce outcomes that were socially optimal. So if full employment was socially desirable—as Keynes for one thought it definitely was—markets could not be left to act alone. Instead, market processes needed to be supplemented by political action of a purposive and deliberate kind.

Markets were not to be abandoned completely. This was not Keynes' view. He was not a Marxist. Markets were simply to be influenced, shaped and indirectly controlled—and they were to be all these things the better to strengthen the effectiveness of their working, and the better to re-legitimate the property relationships of capitalist economies which in the 1930s were in deep economic and political trouble. Out of a particular reading of the causes of the Great Depression, the Keynesian specification for the role of the state came to be one requiring governments to systematically manage levels of demand in the economy as a whole (by their instructions to banks, and by their own spending), in order to keep overall demand at that level which alone could generate and then sustain high and rising levels of employment. It was a specification of how governments could manage capitalist economies, the better to save them from their own excesses, which gave social reformers for an entire generation after 1945 an answer both to classically liberal critics of state action and to Marxist criticisms of capitalism as an economic system. So it was a specification too, like classical liberalism before it, which became for a while the ruling orthodoxy of the age.

THE CLASH OF PARADIGMS

Paradigms in the social sciences, like those in the natural sciences, only sustain their hegemony if they are able intelligently to address the key issues of the day; and while they are so capable, their dominance often seems both inevitable and natural. Keynesianism seemed to be in that position for the first three decades of the post-World War II period. Rates of economic growth in the advanced industrial economies were sufficiently robust as to remove the threat of mass unemployment from the memory of a new generation of workers, and governments used Keynesian understandings of their role to stimulate aggregate demand in their individual economies when unemployment loomed and to lower it when prices began to rise. What Keynesianism seemed to preclude—and what very few people anticipated could ever happen again—was the emergence of a period of economic dislocation in which unemployment *and* prices would rise together: for in such a period governments could not both cut and expand their spending at one and the same time as they would have to do, Keynesian style, to handle each. Yet that is exactly what came to pass in the 1970s. Unemployment began to rise and inflation to soar simultaneously, and the word "soar" is not an exaggeration here. The UK inflation rate soared to well over 20 percent by the middle of the decade. Capitalism (in economies as central to the global system as both the United States and the United Kingdom) was in crisis again—this time, a crisis of stagflation—and so was Keynesianism: publicly rejected by no less than its leading political vehicle, the British Labour Party. Indeed the last Labour prime minister of the Keynesian period, James Callaghan, even went so far as to tell his party conference, amid the United Kingdom's IMF-debt crisis of 1976, that:

> we used to think that you could spend your way out of a recession, and increase employment by cutting taxes and boosting Government spending. I tell you in all candor that that option no longer exists, and that in so far as it ever did exist, it only worked on each occasion since the war by injecting a bigger dose of inflation into the economy, followed by a higher level of unemployment as the next step.
>
> (Callaghan, 1976)

You don't often hear a clearer rejection of the central claims of Keynesianism than that, and certainly not from the leader of a political party committed to the politics of social reform.

Classical liberalism then made its intellectual and political comeback, restored to public legitimacy as a core part of the economic strategy of the Center-Right governments that replaced the Labour Party in power in the United Kingdom in 1979 and drove the Democrats from the White House in 1980. In the era of Margaret Thatcher and Ronald Reagan, a faith in the generally beneficial consequences of unregulated markets returned to center stage; and Keynesians were broadly discredited both for supposedly trying to push the rate of unemployment below what was "natural" in a modern economy, and for privileging demand issues in a capitalist economy over supply-side ones. Keynesianism found itself widely blamed for both the unemployment and the inflation of the 1970s, as though it had somehow created both: blamed by conservative politicians adamant that big and active government inevitably reduced rates of economic growth through the high taxes, excessive welfare provision and over-regulation of private industry that it brought in its wake. Privatization (the selling off of publicly owned industries and firms) and deregulation (the freeing of the private sector from government oversight) became the order of the day, along with new labor codes restricting the rights of trade unions to engage in collective bargaining and to strike, and a general restructuring of the welfare state (both the setting of tighter limits on its growth, and the exposure wherever possible of welfare sector providers to the full force of market competition).

None of this was simply a knee-jerk reaction by public policy-makers to the general crisis of Keynesianism. It should be thought of more as a return to some very core classically liberal economic principles, now reset (as **neo-liberalism**) in a world of welfare capitalisms and increasing global trade. The precise form which the return took varied in different countries and at different times, but the overall pattern was clear. In Margaret Thatcher's hands in the 1980s, Conservative ire was heavily focused on the unproductive nature of public sector employment and the associated supposedly superior productivity of jobs provided by private sector enterprise. Thatcherites talked constantly about the adverse consequences of public sector taxes squeezing out private sector saving, about the way public sector borrowing inevitably increased the price of private sector investment, and about the dangers of public sector welfare provision ultimately generating a permanent underclass of the welfare-dependent unemployed. Two decades later in the America of George W. Bush, all these Thatcherite themes were then reconfigured into a case for the superiority of "trickle-down economics," the argument being that the best way to stimulate job creation in the private sector was to lower taxation in general (so stimulating demand) and to lower upper-level taxes in particular (so encouraging the rich—the "job creators"—to do their job creation, the so-called incentive effect). By then welfare-to-work programs were on the rise on both sides of the Atlantic, with welfare provision increasingly tied to the willingness of welfare recipients to seek work, however badly paid—a policy of welfare retrenchment that was predicated on the view that even low-paid work in the private sector was a better route to long-term prosperity for those caught up in it than any dependence on government welfare provision could ever hope to be.

The general credibility of this "neo-liberal" turn was very high in the 1990s and in the years up to 2007, because in that nearly twenty-year period economic growth proceeded virtually without falter in both the leading neo-liberal economies (the United States and the United Kingdom) and because full employment had returned to both. But the general credibility of a fully deregulated private (especially banking sector-led) economy then took a major hit when the US (and rapidly thereafter the bulk of the global) financial system crashed in the last quarter of 2008, and as across the globe as a whole maybe as many as 50 million people lost their jobs in the prolonged recession that followed. But credibility is not a feature of economic theories that either automatically glues itself to them or is automatically lost. It is something which has to be fought for, and fought over. The need—recognized widely in the finance ministries of all the leading capitalist economies in late 2008, and that included China—that government spending had to play a large and immediate role in limiting the economic damage caused by the collapse of confidence in private sector-based financial institutions, did briefly re-establish public interest in a Keynesian alternative to neo-liberalism. But as the post-2008 recession dragged on, and as the scale of public borrowing continued to be high, neo-liberal economists and conservative politicians bounced back with one other addition to their intellectual equipment: the notion that heavy borrowing stacked up debts for the future, making the children and grandchildren of those now doing the borrowing pay the long-term price. What the 2008 crisis and its fallout have not done is to bring another economic paradigm to dominance. What the crisis and its fallout did instead was to create again a period in which no intellectual paradigm is dominant, and in which the politics of the Center have been accordingly gridlocked by the persistence of profound disagreements between neo-liberals and post-Keynesians. These are disagreements about exactly why the wheels have come off the capitalist bus, and about exactly how best they can be reattached in order to generate another round of economic growth, rising employment and improving standards of life for the mass and generality of those employed in capitalist circuits of production. These are disagreements between paradigms and not just between economists.

This impasse has done one other thing too. It has created the space again to consider whether Marxist explanations of capitalist crises might still yet have something of value to tell us about our contemporary condition and possible likely futures. And Marxism certainly does have something to say. Marxists, unlike classical liberals and Keynesians, rather expect capitalism to be in crisis. Their problem tends to be the reverse one. They have constantly to explain periods of stability and growth in economies in which, from a Marxist perspective, the tension between capital and labor should permanently threaten the capacity of the system to generate sufficient profits and investment to sustain adequate levels of employment and generalized rises in living standards. That tension between capital and labor, if Marx was right, should threaten the ability of capitalists to *accumulate* enough profit if labor is too strong. A strong labor movement will demand high wages and slower processes of work, eroding the scale of profit extraction in the process. Likewise that tension between capital and labor should threaten the ability of capitalists to *realize* their profits if labor is too weak: because weak labor movements lack the capacity to demand high wages and so fail to sustain the demand-side conditions vital to the sale of all the commodities flowing from the factories and offices of capitalism. Marxists, that is, expect capitalist economies to ebb and flow between "crises of accumulation" and "crises of realization"; and expect capitalism to flourish only if the balance between capital and labor is temporarily optimal for them both. (Aglietta, 1979) Much like Goldilocks and the three bears, from a Marxist perspective the capitalist porridge can be too hot, too cold or just about right: but it is normally too hot or too cold.

Armed with this set of understandings, one particular school of contemporary Marxist scholarship—known as the regulation school (Kotz et al., 1994)—has argued of late that post-war core capitalist economies have experienced two prolonged but ultimately fragile periods of class balance: two particular class settlements between capital and labor (what they would call particular "social structures of accumulation") capable of holding at bay the inherent propensity of capitalism to move from crisis to crisis. The first period, after World War II, as we initially saw in Chapter 1, was primarily based on the development of semi-automated manufacturing systems that raised productivity, output and profits on the supply side of the capitalist equation, and on strong labor unions that maintained rising wages, and so an adequate flow of consumers, on the demand side. That growth period—one in which Keynesian demand management played an important balancing role—lasted through into the 1970s. It lasted until that moment at which the productivity gains achievable by Fordist product methods began to level off, and trade union strength began to tip the balance of wages and profits too severely toward the former. The second growth period—the one triggered by the resetting of class relationships under the political leadership of people such as Margaret Thatcher and Ronald Reagan—eventually created another, if more fragile class balance. This one was built on the productivity gains associated with computerization and on the demand conditions associated with the rise of private debt. Strong trade unions and significant wage rises for most workers were not a feature of this second class settlement. As we saw earlier, an increase in the number of family members going out to paid work, an increase in their working hours, and the accumulation of credit card debt by family members as a whole, substituted for the wage rises of the first settlement. And like the first class settlement, the second one also ended, this time in a brief but brutal credit crisis that broke people's confidence in their ability to lend, borrow and spend. What Marxist crisis theory brings to the table, therefore, is the argument that any renewed and sustained period of capitalist economic growth will require the construction of a new class settlement as well as the adoption of appropriate forms of economic policy; and that since the construction of such class settlements inevitably takes time—often decades—we should not expect rapid long-term global economic recovery any time soon.

CHOOSING BETWEEN PARADIGMS

These three ways of understanding capitalism and its potential are so different that at some point it does become necessary to choose between them. One way, of course, is to reject them all and go find a fourth one. There are lots of other takes on capitalism out there in the literature and in the blogosphere if you have the energy for the hunt. Another is to cherry-pick, to create a package of ideas of your own that draw on what you see as the best elements of the traditions we have described. But that cherry-picking will need to be done with caution—creative syntheses can so easily slip into mindless eclecticism if you are not careful—so before doing either of these things (hunting or cherry-picking) perhaps it is worth considering these four strategies for coming to at least a preliminary view of the relative strengths and weaknesses of the three competing paradigms we have laid out here.

One way of choosing between them is to begin with the question of the "market," and to ask yourself some hard questions about the competing claims made for and about it by both its advocates and its critics. Is it the case, as advocates of a libertarian and *laissez-faire* attitude to market regulation normally insist, that markets left to themselves do effectively three things that regulated markets can do only imperfectly at best? (1) They transmit myriads of information to an endless list of economic actors; (2) they so shape the incentive structures of those actors that the collective result is an optimum allocation of scarce economic resources; and in the process (3) they generate a distribution of rewards that is reflective of the usefulness and capacity of each and every market participant. Moreover, do you believe, as so many conservative commentators appear to do, that if you regulate and tax a company, you weaken its capacity for innovation and competition? And is your view of government intervention as negative as theirs: namely that all governments can ultimately do is to redistribute resources from the economically successful to the economically unsuccessful, so raising a whole string of **moral hazard** issues and eating away at key structures of individual and corporate incentives? (Friedman & Friedman, 1980: 9–24)

Or on the contrary, is it your view, in line with those of more progressive commentators, that unregulated markets have a way of degenerating from perfect to imperfect competition, and a propensity to respond not to the full set of human needs but only to the needs of those with purchasing power, and/or to needs artificially created by corporate advertising? Is it your view that, left to themselves, markets are great engines of inequality rather than equality, eroding level playing fields within and between generations, so that the children of the rich and the children of the poor find themselves on different life trajectories by virtue of their birth and circumstances rather than as a consequence of their own distinct abilities and characters? And where are you on the Keynes' question? Do markets automatically settle at levels of full employment without the guiding hand of the interventionist state, and do businesses left with only the lightest of public regulation behave well or behave badly? Is what is good for General Motors automatically the same thing as what is good for America? If, broadly speaking, the first list of claims seem stronger to you than the second, then this might well be the time to go read some Adam Smith or some Milton Friedman. But if not, if on the contrary you see some mileage in the notion that negative freedoms need to be supplemented by positive ones, then maybe the focus of your reading should shift: certainly to Keynes, possibly even to Marx.

A *second way* of choosing is to reflect more broadly on the conceptual apparatus each tradition offers you as a way of understanding the world—both your personal world and the more general one around you. The choices here, as listed in Table 4.1, are fairly clear.

Classical liberalism suggests to you that your characteristic categories of analysis should include "the atomized individual," "individual rationality," "the market," "private property," "personal freedom" and a "social contract." Armed with these,

Table 4.1 Characteristic categories of analysis, statements and models of the global order

Classical liberalism	Social reformism	Marxism
Characteristic categories		
individual	mixed economy	modes of production
rationality	status groups	capitalism
market	dominant elites	classes
rights	reform	social structures of
liberty		accumulation
social contract		revolution
Characteristic statements		
Society is the sum of self-interested individuals in the rational pursuit of private goals	Modern society is immensely complex, but open to incremental reform and democratic management	Life is dominated by the contradictions and instabilities of capitalism, and requires revolutionary change
Models of the global order		
traditional–modern	North–South	core–periphery

according to classical liberals, you should be able to make sense of the main economic and social processes going on around you. Marxism offers you a different set of categories of analysis to use to make sense of that same world. It offers you things such as "modes of production," "social classes," "exploitation," even "social structures of accumulation" and "social revolution." Social reformism suggests you define the economy as "managed" or "mixed (private and public)," that you see social divisions as matters of "status" as well as of "class," and that you understand politics as a matter of "reform" led by significant "elites." Each tradition will also give you a particular view of the global order. Classical liberalism will suggest you divide the world into "traditional" and "modern" societies, with capitalism as embodying the best of the modern to which less capitalist-organized economies and societies need to (and will) aspire. Marxism tends to see the global order as divided between "core" and "peripheral" economies, with that division prone to reproduction over time as surpluses built up in peripheral societies end up enhancing profitability (and living standards) in the core. The tradition we have labeled here as social reformism tends to offer you a view of the global order as one divided between a conceptual "North" of developed capitalisms and a "South" of less developed ones, with uneven exchange between North and South benefiting the North unless international agencies intervene to at least partially level the global playing field.

Third, it is worth reflecting at some point on the general questions normally raised when considering the relative strengths of particular intellectual paradigms. Those questions characteristically explore the explanatory capacity of each tradition under at least five headings: their explanatory power, their reach, their coherence, their openness and their impact. The questions are listed here as a general checklist to which it is probably wise regularly to return. The *explanatory power* of an intellectual tradition is normally measured by its capacity to handle evidence and its clarity on what would constitute significant counterfactual evidence, and by the number of interesting and important topics that lie unexamined outside its explanatory reach. That *explanatory reach* is best measured by the range of issues the tradition can explain, by the depth and complexity of the explanations offered, and by the scale and importance of the things ignored or left unexplained. The *explanatory coherence* of an intellectual tradition is best measured by the number and quality of linkages in its characteristic explanatory chain, and by the degree to which those linkages stretch back with ease to some core organizing concepts. The *explanatory openness* of an intellectual tradition measures its capacity to absorb new circumstances, or lines of research, and how well it can articulate with other bodies of explanation without losing its original coherence; and the *explanatory impact* of an intellectual tradition is normally best measured by the social consequences of applying its precepts to real circumstances, by the nature of the winners and losers in that process, and by the interests it privileges and the values it serves. All that is a tall order to handle, of course, but as a first stab you might choose to think about how each of the three intellectual traditions we have just examined can explain important things at which we have not yet looked. How well would each deal with gender relationships, for example, or with climate change, or with the persistence of racial discrimination?

But the big problem about those general questions is that they are really tough ones to answer in any quick and easy way, so there may be a *fourth* strategy for choice here, depending on what time of day you are reading this particular chapter: namely procrastination! The intellectual and political choices we make are always contingent on experience and data, so why not

Table 4.2 Theoretical options: criteria for choice

Explanatory power

    Capacity to handle evidence
    Degree of vulnerability to facts
    Clarity on counter-factual tests
    Number of special exceptions being canvassed

Explanatory reach

    Range of issues covered
    Scale and importance of matters ignored/unexplained
    Degree of depth—status of unexplained independent variable
    Degree to which as range expands, coherence diminishes

Explanatory coherence

    The number and quality of linkages in the explanatory chain
    The number of unlinked elements in the explanation
    The degree to which linkages stretch back to an organizing concept
    The elegance and clarity of the explanation

Explanatory openness

    Capacity to absorb new circumstances/new lines of research
    Openness to articulation with additional lines of explanation
    Degree to which that openness is compatible with original coherence
    Openness to criticism and to self-reflection

Explanatory impact

    The social consequences of applying its prescriptions
    The pattern of winners and losers associated with its prescriptions
    The interests privileged
    The values structuring the approach

momentarily at least decide to postpone the big one. Why not leave the status of capitalism still in contention by putting off the choice between intellectual paradigms until we have explored together one final set of questions about the performance of capitalism to date. These are questions not so much about its character, history and internal dynamics as about the *effects* of capitalism on a whole range of economic, social, political and cultural dimensions of our modern condition. Rather than asking if capitalism is good or bad in some absolute sense, as both its advocates and its severest critics tend to do, it is worth exploring instead whether the arrival and development of capitalism on the historical stage has been broadly positive or broadly negative in its impact. So let us now ask that question—the impact question— understanding that our answer to it could well have long-term consequences for our choice of intellectual paradigm as well as more short-term consequences for the way we immediately choose to vote and to act.

FOR FURTHER EXPLORATION

I suggest you start by reading Bottomore (1985), Kay (2003) and Wolff & Renick (2012); before turning (for a fuller introduction to the individual traditions) to Friedman & Friedman (1980), Hutton (1994) and Harvey (2014).

5

CAPITALISM AND ITS CONSEQUENCES

Making a judgment call between competing claims about the nature and potential of economies organized on capitalist lines will be easier for each of us when we have gathered a clearer sense of capitalism's impact on a series of things that matter to us. Quite what those are may well differ between us, so this is one point in the argument about capitalism and its potential that might benefit from a brief moment of reflection about criteria and measurement.

It is normal, in governing circles, to initially measure economic success in terms of hard numerical things such as GDP growth, employment levels and living standards; and quite properly so, because those things are important. But simple GDP numbers can also distort, giving weight to things that we may not value/approve of (such as excessive advertising or bank speculation) while failing to capture things that we do value (such as security, community and the beauty of the natural environment). Indeed, the recent widespread recognition of such limits has stimulated a proliferation of new ways of measuring economic progress and success, ways that do not so much break with this formal reliance on GDP measures as seek to supplement them. Perhaps the best known and most widely used of these new indicators is the United Nations' *Human Development Index* (HDI): an index that adds to simple measures of GDP indices of life expectancy, length of education and per capita income. The UN also issues an Inequality-Adjusted HDI that is more sensitive than the original to dimensions of gender inequality and poverty. But the UN is only one player here. There are many others. In 2008, for example, the French government commissioned a report from three leading economists that combined measures of current well-being with assessments of long-term sustainability. (Stiglitz, 2008) In 2009 the London-based New Economics Foundation produced a set of National Accounts of Well-being that explicitly attempted to capture "how people feel and experience their lives, help to define our notions of national progress, success and what we value as a society." (NEF, 2009: 3; also Frey & Stutzer, 2002: 36–43) In 2014, leading academics at Harvard followed that with their own Social Progress Index that ranked New Zealand first, ranked the United Kingdom thirteenth and had the United States just outside the top fifteen. (Porter, 2014) Indeed there is now a new and growing academic literature—Richard Layard called it "a new science" (Layard, 2005)—on the economics of happiness. (Frey, 2010: 13–14) We will have cause to draw on that literature later in this chapter, but for the moment all we need note is that the proliferation of such measures underscores just how complex and difficult a matter it is to judge the success or failures of capitalism in general, or of different national capitalisms in particular: but judge them we must.

So potentially, the list of possible measures that we might use here is truly vast, but for our purposes it makes sense to focus on just a few: first on capitalism's impact on general living standards over time, then on its impact on various forms of social division, and finally on its impact on both private forms of fulfillment and public forms of politics. What we are going to find in each case is significant progress over the long period on all the key indicators we deploy—we are going to find that, in this sense, capitalism genuinely works—but that it always works better for some than for others, and that it always works with a degree of impermanence, with an unavoidable propensity for its benefits to ebb as well as to flow.

LIVING STANDARDS IN THE PAST: CORE CAPITALISMS

As must be clear from the last chapter, there are very few things on which Adam Smith, Karl Marx and John Maynard Keynes would probably have agreed, but one of them is this: all of them were conscious of the economic dynamism that came with the resetting of economic life on capitalist lines. Even Marx and Engels recognized that, as they put it, "the bourgeoisie, during its rule of scarce one hundred years, has created more massive and more colossal productive forces than have all preceding generations together." (Marx & Engels, 1848: 39) The results of that dynamism are everywhere evident in all the available data, which show that *the overall impact of capitalism on per capita income has been both striking and unprecedented.* One major example should make the point. When in the 1990s the doyen of growth accounting, Angus Maddison, examined the available data on long-term rates of economic growth and per capita income, he found (as others had done before him) that "between 1820 and 1989 there was a substantial increase in real income in all countries outside Africa," but that "the rates of growth in these countries varied considerably" with "a clear divergence in performance over the long run." It was the countries that had reset their economies on capitalist lines that, in Maddison's data, "had the highest incomes and the fastest long-term growth." Between 1820 and 1989, as he put it, in "the capitalist core economies . . . average real income rose thirteen-fold." Whereas, by contrast, his group of non-capitalist African countries "had the lowest income level" so that the average per capita income there now "is not very different from that of the capitalist core 120 years ago." And for Maddison, as again for others, the differential performance between global areas on per capita income was not to be explained by changes in population size and structure. It was to be explained by the differential ability of their economies to mobilize land, labor, capital and enterprise in the pursuit of economic growth. (Maddison, 1995: 119) It was to be explained by capitalism.

To this hymn of praise for capitalism as a growth machine, however, we do need to add several important caveats. The first is that the capacity of economies organized on fully capitalist lines to generate high levels of per capita income is at best less than a century old. *Capitalism's capacity to generate affluence, that is, is a very recent phenomenon.* As we have already noted more than once, prior to World War II general living standards even in the core capitalisms (in the United States, Western Europe and Japan) were low. Necessarily so, because any rise in general living standards requires the emergence of an economy in which the productivity of labor is high; and prior to the post-1939 dissemination of semi-automated production systems of the Fordist variety, the productivity of labor even at the core of the global capitalist system was never high by modern standards. Prior to 1939, most production even in the United States relied as much on human effort as it did on machinery; and there is only so much output that a man/woman can generate per hour if using their energy and muscle power alone. And where machinery was deployed in early capitalisms, it was (by modern standards) only of a pre-liminary and primitive kind. Prior to 1939, in each core capitalist economy large swathes of the population remained on the land, where technology was slow to modernize; and their industrial sectors relied for their main source of energy on coal that was still largely dug out of the ground by human sweat. It was only after 1939 (and initially under the imperatives of global warfare) that mass production took off on a large and sustained scale, and that in consequence core capitalist economies were suddenly able, from their now much more extensive manufacturing sectors, to produce large numbers of consumer goods with very little labor input relative to the mass of goods produced. But then the problem at the heart of the core capitalisms shifted. Instead of there being too few goods available to raise everybody's level of consumption, now the flow of goods ran the risk of outstripping the ability of the mass of consumers to buy them. But buy them they did, in increasing volume year after year in the post-World War II period, as the demand side of the capitalist equation was strengthened (as we saw earlier) by full employment and rising wages for the first post-war generations of workers in core capitalist economies, and then by the longer hours worked by, and the greater availability of personal credit to, the generations that followed.

LIVING STANDARDS IN THE PAST: OUTSIDE THE CORE

To any easy notion that this more modern form of capitalism automatically generates affluence, we also need to add a second caveat: namely that *in global terms, and thus far, any generalized affluence produced by capitalism has been a very restricted phenomenon.* The prosperity now known in core capitalisms still remains to be achieved both in economies previously organized on communist lines and (more significantly for our purposes) in the bulk of non-communist economies outside the capitalist core. The most rapid and successful rates of economic growth in the immediate post-World War II period occurred within what W. J. Baumol rightly termed the "convergence club." (Baumol, 1994: 64) As US per capita living standards rose after 1945, living standards in Western European economies converged on them. Over a three-decade period, Western Europe played catch-up on America by adopting American production techniques—and for geo-political reasons, as we have seen, Western Europe was followed in this regard first by Japan and later by South Korea, both of whom were invited to join this emerging "convergence club" and both of whom benefited greatly from American-provided/induced foreign direct investment as they did so. But for so long as the Cold War persisted, no other national economy was invited to join in this convergence. Nor was any other national economy able to force its way in. On the contrary, the pattern of post-war convergence of living standards in the conceptual "North," striking as it was, left general living standards in the rest of the non-communist world largely unchanged.

Largely unchanged, and possibly even blocked: because for so long as Western colonial control prevailed, adverse terms of trade between the First World and the Third World were an important source of rising living standards in the core capitalisms themselves. That is why, until well into the 1960s, it was possible to argue with some credibility that the development in the core economies of the global economic system actually depended to a significant degree on the *under-development* of their Third World suppliers of raw materials and cheap labor, or at least that it depended on a holding back of industrial development in Third World economies wherever that potential development threatened suppliers based in the capitalist core. (Gunder Frank, 1967) It is true that some economies outside the core challenged their global subordination for a while—Brazil and Mexico in the 1950s certainly did—by pursuing strategies of ISI behind tariff walls of the kind that the United States had used in the nineteenth century to protect its fledgling industries from excessive British competition. But ultimately even they failed to break entirely the stranglehold of global economic inequality put in place, initially under colonial control, in the years between 1870 and 1914. The data generated by Giovanni Arrighi on this is very clear. Writing just at the end of the Cold War, his analysis suggested that "after more than thirty years of developmental efforts of all kinds, the gaps that separate the incomes of the East and the South from those of the West/North are today wider than ever before." To sustain that claim, Arrighi created a measure of per capita income in what he called the "organic core of the capitalist world

Table 5.1 Comparative economic performance in the "South"

	1938	1948	1960	1970	1980	1988
I. Latin America	19.5	14.4	16.7	15.5	19.8	10.6
I.1 Excluding Brazil	23.8	16.2	19.6	17.3	21.1	9.7
II. Middle East & North Africa	n.a.	n.a.	11.5	8.1	11.1	7.1
II.I "Turkey & Egypt"	14.9	13.0	12.8	7.7	8.1	5.6
III. Sub-Saharan Africa						
III.I Western & Eastern	n.a.	n.a.	3.6	3.4	4.7	0.6
III.II South & Central	25.2	18.3	10.5	11.3	n.a.	6.1
IV. South Asia	8.2	7.5	3.6	2.8	2.0	1.8
V. Southeast Asia	n.a.	n.a.	6.6	3.8	5.7	3.7
V.I "Indonesia & Philippines"	6.0	n.a.	6.4	2.8	4.6	2.3

Note: The figures represent GNP per capita of region or aggregate divided by the GNP per capita of the organic core times 100. The organic core are the countries whose GNP per capita was earlier recorded in Table 2.1.

Source: Arrighi (1991: 49)

economy" (by which he meant Western Europe, North America and Australia/New Zealand) and then compared that income to the income prevalent in the rest of the world system in a series of key years. The results make pretty depressing reading for those who think capitalism raises all boats. What the results actually show is the persistence of combined but uneven economic development over time right up to the end of the Cold War.

CAPITALISM AND LIVING STANDARDS NOW

All of the above helps explain the novelty and importance of what is happening globally now, but also underscores its potential risks for the labor movements of core capitalist economies in the conceptual "North."

With the collapse of communism and the thickening of global inter-connections between national economies, a full-scale capitalist "catch-up" is again underway—but one which this time is not restricted by US geo-political concerns. The prime mover on this occasion is definitely China, whose political system still remains communist but whose economy (as we saw) is increasingly capitalist in nature. A new large, increasingly self-confident and powerful Chinese middle class is driving the full-scale industrialization of what was once an almost exclusively peasant society, in the process altering the entire international division of labor between "northern" core and "southern" periphery. And China is not alone in this regard. The Chinese economy is simply one of several—one of the BRIC economies—joined by Brazil, Russia and India in a headlong dash for growth. Other "southern" economies are raising output, productivity and living standards too: Argentina and Chile among others in South America, Indonesia and the Philippines in Asia, and Israel in the Middle East.

Indeed it is now easier to point to areas of economic under-development globally than once it was, precisely because global development is currently so much more extensive than in the immediate post-World War II era. Africa remains, for the moment at least, largely a lost continent in economic terms (Page, 2014); and Middle Eastern political turmoil overshadows economic development even in oil-rich producing countries such as Iran and Iraq. But even so, capitalist development is underway again on a global scale, bringing renewed pressure on average wages in the conceptual "North," and leaving full-scale economic development less and less a monopoly of the original core capitalisms. The results, in terms of living standards, are however still only modest. Things outside the core capitalisms are currently not quite as bad as once they were, but not by much. As the latest ILO report has it,

> The number of working poor continues to decline globally, albeit at a slower rate than during previous decades. In 2013, 375 million workers (or 11.9 percent of total employment) are estimated to live on less than US$1.25 a day and [as we noted earlier] 839 million workers (or 26.7 percent of total employment) have to cope on US$2 a day or less.
>
> (ILO, 2014: 12)

For all the recent growth of the global economy, "40 percent of the world's population—2.8 billion people—[are still] living on $2–$10 a day (measured in 2005 purchasing power parity terms)" (Donnan et al., 2014) and almost half the world's population—some 3 billion people—are still struggling to survive on less than $2.50 a day.

One final feature of generalized living standards is important as a third caveat in this discussion of the impact of capitalism on economic growth: namely the currently *precarious nature of rising living standards even in core capitalisms*. It may well prove to be that, in the conceptual "North," the baby boomer generation has been a particularly blessed one, enjoying for a period (and uniquely in the overall story of capitalism) a confidence in the steady improvement in the material quality of their lives that their children and grandchildren will not know. It is true that the late baby boomers, those born in the 1950s, had a tough decade (or decade and a half) after the oil crisis of 1973 brought the generalized expansion of Western capitalist economies to a temporary halt. It certainly took until the 1990s to put the US and UK economies back onto a sustained growth path, and the economic burden of unification made that return to growth slower still for the hitherto rapidly expanding West German economy. But nonetheless, across the core of the global system as a whole—with the exception of Japan which has been uniquely stuck in low growth rates for more than two decades after its own financial crisis in 1992—living standards rose again for most people from the 1990s until the financial crisis of 2008. There was always an extensive underclass of the genuine poor even then. Poverty rates in the United States never fell below 11 percent even at the height of the Clinton-era boom; and income inequality was always greater in the LMEs we listed in Chapter 2 than it was in the CMEs. But after 2008, as the financial crisis gave way to a generalized recession, poverty rates rose again in a dramatic fashion across the entire industrialized world, real wages stagnated for most people living in core capitalist economies, and unemployment and job insecurity returned to those labor forces on a significant scale. A degree of economic security known for a generation in the "North," and the certainty that living standards would rise generation on generation, was suddenly known and certain no longer.

So it seems best to say, of capitalism, that its great claim to fame is its dynamism. Capitalism is the great growth machine, as its champions regularly proclaim. But very few people benefited initially from that growth. Many more benefit now, to capitalism's great credit. But it is still the case that, for most people on this planet, living standards remain very low; and where they are not, that recently they have become again markedly less secure.

CAPITALISM AND CLASS

So far in this chapter, we have considered per capita income as though, within societies based on capitalist economies, all incomes are equal: but of course they are not. Capitalism emerged as a way of organizing economic life into societies—normally feudal ones—that were themselves stratified. Indeed, capitalism arrived precisely as a new social class emerged, of people—normally men—who survived by organizing the production, distribution and sale of commodities. Capitalism, that is, emerged in societies already divided into social classes. It then brought new social classes into play; and over time it changed the meaning of what it meant to be a member of a particular social class. So as with living standards, so too with social divisions—capitalism had a huge impact and the question, of course, is exactly what that impact was.

Here the nineteenth-century writings of Marx and Weber are a useful—and still a very conventional—starting point. The two agreed that capitalism, as it spread first from agriculture and trade into industry and finance, eroded and ultimately replaced class divisions of a pre-capitalist kind. Aristocracies and peasantries persisted into the modern period, but they stopped being the main form of social division once a capitalist way of organizing the economy had gained traction. Indeed, early capitalisms such as the United States and United Kingdom were "early" in part precisely because feudal class structures had been either already transformed (as in the English case) or avoided altogether (in the American one); and later capitalisms (not least Germany and Japan) were "late" in part because of the residual presence of strong aristocracies and large-scale peasantries in each of their social formations. What Marx and Weber agreed on was that capitalism created new social classes that came to overwhelm, both in size and social importance, their feudal predecessors. Capitalism, that is, rose alongside the emergence of what we would instantly recognize as a *middle class* (a social category reproducing itself through successful economic entrepreneurship) and an equally recognizable *working class* (a social category of men and women selling their labor power for wages and no longer reproducing themselves by working the land to produce food that they themselves then consumed). Some of that working class did work the land—capitalism came with an agrarian working class as well as an industrial one—but the produce which agrarian workers generated by their labor was itself sold, as the private property of the social class who employed them, a class of capitalist farmers.

What Marx and Weber did not agree on, however, was what came next. Marx thought that fierce competition between small-scale capitalists would rapidly drive all but the most successful down into the working class: that the future of class divisions in capitalism would be one of class simplification, class polarization, and the intensification of class struggles between an ever expanding working class and an ever shrinking capitalist one. Weber, by contrast, recognizing the strength and persistence of the large bureaucratic structures emerging as capitalism developed—

large private sector bureaucratically organized firms, large state agencies, even large military ones—was convinced that over time the middle class would grow, the working class would shrink, and the class tensions between them would slowly abate. In terms of the subsequent trajectory of class relationships in core capitalisms, Weber certainly got the better of the debate between the two. The contemporary class structure of advanced capitalisms now has a complex middle class, a transformed working class and residues of their pre-capitalist past (aristocracies and peasantries) all mixed up together—class structures that lend themselves more easily to analyses derived from Weberian scholarship than from its Marxist equivalent.

So what do we now know about capitalism and class? We know that capitalism did not do away with classes, that rather it replaced old classes with new ones. We know that, over time and in the core capitalisms at least, the severity of the battle for scarce resources between these new classes eased, as (through waves of investment and innovation triggered by capitalist competition and the pursuit of profit) the productivity of capitalism increased the stock of available resources over which the classes would fight. And we know that, as levels of commodity consumption grew in the conceptual "North", and as the labor process associated with the production of commodities became increasingly mechanized and thus marginally easier on the workers involved in it, people's sense of themselves as members of particular societies progressively shifted. It shifted away from thinking of themselves as members of mutually incompatible producing classes, toward thinking of themselves as individual members of a society-wide collection of consumers. Thus far at least, being a member of a class—particularly a subordinate one— has never become so easy (even in the core capitalisms) that people fail to include it in their own sense of themselves—in their own self-definition. But nonetheless, what Marx had so confidently expected when surveying the brutality of life in early industrial capitalism (that being a member of the working class would be so horrendous as to drown out all other forms of self-definition) has simply failed to happen. Marx thought advanced capitalism and intensified class struggle would go together. He failed to see that the class struggles he anticipated as occurring at the very core of the capitalist system would be moved out to the system's edge; and that because they were (as we saw in Chapter 3) a space would open up in the core economies of the global system within which a moderate form of working-class politics could be consolidated. If we want to understand class relations in the newly emerging capitalist economies of the "South," Karl Marx still has much to tell us. But for the class relations of the capitalist core, it is often more productive to turn to Max Weber.

Several features of class structure, class experience and class relationships stand out as predominant in core capitalisms. In terms of class structure, the number of men and women working in factories and fields has declined, and the number working in offices and in service occupations has risen. In early capitalism, office work was the monopoly of the privileged few: it carried clear middle-class status. Now the working conditions and terms of employment of many office and service workers suggest that we have a new and emerging white-collar working class to set alongside a shrinking factory-based manual one. In terms of class structure too, the bureaucratic developments that Weber anticipated have indeed produced large numbers of middle managers and state employees—effectively two new middle classes, one employed in private industry and one employed by the state.

People's experience as members of these new working and middle classes is not the same as it was for their equivalents generations ago. General living standards are higher, as we have seen, and the degree of welfare provision—the safety net underpinning employment should paid work be lost through age, disability, injury or recession—is now greater than once it was (particularly in both the "conservative" and "social democratic" welfare capitalisms discussed in Chapter 2). But the underlying reality remains: that life chances are fixed by position in unequal labor markets, and that social relationships across class boundaries are still far rarer than are social relationships within social classes themselves. Over time, as in the past, some people still experience social mobility—moving between social classes both up and down—but as bureaucracies have grown, the rags-to-riches kind of social mobility evident in Victorian England has become rarer. People move socially, if they move at all, normally only onto the next rung of the social ladder. And where inequalities in the remuneration associated with particular labor markets widen—that is, as income inequality within any one generation grows—the scale of social mobility diminishes. Indeed, as we will discuss more fully in the next chapter, income and wealth inequality is currently high and growing in leading capitalist economies of the US and UK kind; and because it is, levels of social mobility are currently higher in the welfare capitalisms of Western Europe and Canada than they are in the traditional home of the American Dream.

Class relations in less developed capitalisms remain to date far closer to the original Marxist model than they do in the well-established capitalisms of the North. The labor processes associated with the production of manufactured commodities in places such as China, Brazil, India and Russia remain harsh and underpaid by "northern" standards. The machinery in use there is often as technologically sophisticated as in the most advanced factories of North America and Western Europe, but the hours of work remain longer, the intensity of work more demanding, and levels of pay still significantly less. That is so in part, as we saw in more detail in Chapter 3, because workers in many of the BRIC economies are still fighting for labor rights that workers in core capitalisms won years before. Indeed workers in core capitalisms are often fighting to retain those rights at precisely the moment that workers in the South are seeking to win them for the first time. In Latin America in the decades either side of the millennium, those struggles sent most governments away to the Center-Left (or in Venezuela to the hard Left), but no such shift occurred in former communist countries where labor rights remain limited and denied. What appears to be emerging—both in post-communist Russia and in still formally communist China—is a strong but still limited entrepreneurial middle class of a conventional Victorian kind, plus a large working class that is equally Victorian in the limited scale of its civil and industrial rights. As we noted at the end of Chapter 3, whether a revamped Victorian capitalism will win out in the South and spread North, or whether welfare capitalism will survive in the North and spread South, is the big class issue of the day; but either way, the choice between those two outcomes points to the continuing centrality of class relationships to any society that bases itself on a capitalist form of economic organization.

CAPITALISM AND GENDER

Class divisions are not the only ones, of course, that set people apart and predetermine for them different patterns of life. Nor are they, from many points of view, even the main source of those differences. You might think they were, if all you read were the early documents on capitalism as an economic system—be that *The Wealth of Nations* or *The Communist Manifesto*. For both those documents are largely silent on what is possibly the other main source of social differentiation, that of gender. Marx and Engels did write at least one important pamphlet on that topic (*The Origins of the Family, Private Property and the State*) and issues of gender equality were front and center to the writings of Mary Wollstonecraft within a generation of Adam Smith, and to some of those of John Stuart Mill two generations later. But nonetheless and in general, the scholarship that has come down to us to explain the nature and impact of capitalism has, until very recently, treated questions of gender as secondary and minor, if they treated them at all.

That should appall us, but it should not surprise us, for capitalism emerged into a world that was already heavily patriarchal in its practices and culture, and that patriarchy visibly extended into its early intellectual strata as well as into its main property-owning classes. In pre-capitalist Europe, as in societies across the globe stretching back down the centuries, women had invariably been subordinated to the menfolk with whom they lived, vulnerable to male dominance in large measure because of their perennial exposure, from early puberty on, to the regularity and rigor of childbirth and lactation. Not all pre-industrial societies were patriarchal, but the vast majority of them were. In those, men ruled and women served; and though that did not exclude women from involvement in the production of food and the tending of animals, it did mean that they combined those tasks with the bearing and rearing of children, and did so normally under the general supervision of men.

Early capitalism did not fundamentally alter the basic distribution of power between the sexes, but it did fundamentally alter the economic and social terrain on which those power relationships were played out, and it did over time reset the character of the key institution of patriarchal control, namely the family.

The pre-capitalist European feudal family, normally rurally based, was the site of both production and reproduction. The family as a whole, not simply the internally dominant father, was the basic unit of production, as well as being the site for what Eli Zaretsky once called "the natural processes of eating, sleeping, sexuality and cleaning." (Zaretsky 1986: 12–13) But capitalism ultimately changed that. Over time it separated home from work, and began to privilege—both in rewards and in social significance—the work done in factories and offices over work done at home. Early capitalism took work to the household—early textile production was often a cottage industry. Even today in parts of the developing world basic textile production still goes on within the domestic setting; and in that context, every family member, including the women, work the looms. Early on too, as factories and mines developed, women and children found themselves as exposed—and sometimes more exposed—to wage labor as their menfolk, because their labor was cheaper. But over time, as male workers organized and pressured governments to exclude women from paid employment, a separation opened up between work and home that was heavily gendered.

Men "went out to work" and earned a wage that was meant to sustain the entire family. Women "stayed home" and were not paid, and were said therefore "not to work." They did work, of course. They worked very hard, bearing and raising children, feeding and clothing their men, and looking after parents as they aged: work that was vital to the reproduction of the labor power on which the capitalist production of commodities depended. Indeed when the "market" value of such work was calculated for the United Kingdom in 1997, it effectively doubled the size of the economy's GDP. (R. Adams, 1997) But nonetheless and over time—as the culture of capitalism continued to privilege the production of commodities and to label only wage labor as "work"—the work of women in the home became privately invisible and publicly unvalued. Married women with children were particularly prone by the 1950s to "stay home," in the process becoming increasingly financially and psychologically dependent on the men who left them each day to "go out to work."

Even in the first phase of industrial capitalism, however, not all women were excluded from paid labor, in spite of the best efforts of labor unions and middle-class reformers to have it so. Working-class women may have ultimately been excluded from the mines and the ironworks, but they were never fully excluded from the textile factories or the farms. Black women worked in the cotton fields of the American South. Both they and young European working-class women, prior to their childbearing years, were still extensively employed as domestic servants and as childminders in middle-class households: domestic service remained, in fact, the largest occupational category after mining in the UK economy until well into the 1930s. And by then, middle-class women on both sides of the Atlantic had fought for, and won, the right to work as semi-professionals in both education and in medicine: caring professions that were not that distant in either content or role from those characteristic of the childcare responsibilities and the tending-of-the-old that awaited most women at home.

But in the process of carving out these spaces for paid employment, three elements of an older patriarchy remained in place to structure the participation of women in the newly established capitalist labor markets. One was the loss of some traditionally female occupational monopolies—not least midwifery—to the new and expanding male profession of medicine. A second was the heavy concentration of women in just a limited number of occupations, where they worked almost exclusively only with other women: job segregation by gender was, as it remains, commonplace in early capitalism. A third element was the persistence of the gendering of the managerial hierarchies to which, as workers, women answered. Women worked under male supervision, and rarely the other way round. Capitalism and patriarchy went together easily in the early stage of industrial development, and the residues of that patriarchy are everywhere evident today.

Certain things have recently changed, of course, at least in the core capitalisms of North America and Western Europe. Capitalism there, if not yet to the same degree elsewhere, has adapted to the rising power of women. A quiet social revolution now divides us in the conceptual "North" from the blatant sexism of even the immediate past. Some of that revolution was capitalism's own doing. The production and sale of various forms of birth control became a profitable activity in its own right by the 1960s, with the arrival of the "pill" giving women for the first time greater control over the timing and number of their children. The major wars of the twentieth century—fought between leading capitalist powers—brought women into the labor force as never before; and though many of those women were then pushed back into unpaid domestic production in the years immediately following the end of hostilities, the full employment and welfare provision of the post-World War II era left women by the 1960s not simply more in control of their bodies but also better educated and a vital source of much-needed labor power. The subsequent "deindustrialization" of many of the core capitalist economies then compounded the effect of these changes by reducing the number of routine working-class jobs traditionally done only by men; and the post-1973 general stagnation of wages in these core capitalisms then made it increasingly vital—if family living standards were to rise—that both adults went out to paid employment of some kind.

By the end of the twentieth century in consequence, the traditional "male breadwinner model" that had kept most married women with children out of the paid labor force as late as the 1950s had largely gone. By 2010, half the paid labor force in the United States were women. Most married women with children now return to paid work as the children go to school; and across the Protestant parts of the advanced capitalist world—if not yet the Catholic parts—the traditional family unit (male worker, stay-at-home mother, and 2.4 children) has increasingly given way to a multiplicity of family forms. In the United States in 1960, 70 percent of all families with children were of the male breadwinner kind. By 2007, 70 percent of all such families were of the two-income variety. Divorce—so frowned upon and rare in the 1930s—had become by century's end the fate of one American marriage in two; and one-third of all children in the United States were by then living in one-parent families, the vast majority of which were headed by a working mother.

That is not to say, however, that capitalism as it has advanced has washed patriarchy away. Far from it. The property relationships and political rights of advanced capitalist societies are indeed now largely gender free. The rights of men and women there are largely equal. But away from the public square, even in advanced capitalist societies patriarchal patterns remain both ubiquitous and tenacious. The social division within the household remains heavily gendered. Women, by becoming half the paid labor force, have to a large degree simply adopted a *double burden*: the double burden of performing paid labor while still retaining prime responsibility for the domestic care of both the young and the old. Their "new men" do more childcare than did their fathers, but still in most families they do not do as much childcare as do the women with whom they live, married or not. Nor is the world of paid work yet organized to make the *balancing of work and family* easy for either adult. Hours of work in factories and offices remains out of sync with hours of schooling, and the rights of parents to work flexible hours remain limited/entirely absent even in core capitalisms where other forms of welfare provision are well-developed. What is not absent even in welfare capitalisms are *glass ceilings* that leave women earning less than men overall, and more prone to see their skills underutilized (and their pay diminished) as they returned to paid work after "having their family." What is not absent is the continued gender patterning of part-time work (as more women "choose" work hours most compatible with their childcare role than do the men with whom they live). Moreover, even the most advanced industrial capitalisms remain blighted by *male violence on women*, and by an ever more heavily sexualized culture. We are as far away as we have ever been from a world in which men dance as cheerleaders on the sidelines of a sporting event played exclusively by women—as women now do in the United States at football games played by men—and until we get to that condition it seems worth characterizing even advanced capitalisms as societies that combine economic and gender inequality in ever more complex and embedded ways.

CAPITALISM AND THE QUALITY OF LIFE

Which is not to say, however, that capitalism has somehow failed to improve the lives of all of us fortunate enough to live in the core of the global system. Capitalism has certainly profoundly altered—and ultimately for the better—conditions of life in economies and societies long organized on its basis. Capitalism's separation of home and work has created, for the first time in human history, the emergence of a social space in which large numbers of people are free to pursue their private goals and ambitions; and the recently enhanced productivity of its core economic processes has provided the material goods on a large scale which alone allow those private ambitions to grow and flourish. The emergence of this private space is something that we should both recognize and celebrate. This kind of privacy only became possible because the amount of socially necessary labor time spent in production actually went down, and it was only generalized to the mass of people as the productivity of all of them was enhanced by the application of machinery to production. In that "space" it was possible for the first time for large sections of the working population—and not just a privileged leisured elite—to develop a personal and family life free of the immediate demands of work and production. When movies and television series these days do "time travel," taking us back to life in the past as it was supposed to be, they so often fail to realize that the individual autonomy that their contemporary audience so takes for granted is actually of very recent origin and of capitalist design.

The fact that we are even discussing the quality of life for the bulk of modern populations is a measure of how much capitalism, in its full development, has changed the human condition. Life for most people in pre-capitalist societies was primitive, brutal and short. It was also heavily communal. Life for most people in the factories of early capitalism was only marginally better; but in the last seventy years (in the lifetime, that is, of the oldest of the baby boomers) all that has significantly changed. Life expectancy itself is now much higher in core capitalisms than it was in previous generations: in the United States in 2010, for example, 76.2 years for men and 81.1 for women, when only a half a century ago those numbers would have been only 65.6 and 71.1. (Infoplease, 2014) People in fully developed capitalist economies have access to leisure time, to a quantity and quality of commodities, to a set of public services (from education to health care), and to quality time with friends and family that was literally beyond the imagination of most people only four/five generations ago. As Peter Berger put it in making the case for capitalism and personal liberation, "given the social and cultural bases of western civilization, capitalism is the necessary but not sufficient condition for the continuing reality of individual autonomy." (Berger, 1986: 109) Necessary but—significantly— not sufficient. Even he thought that "capitalism requires institutions that balance the anonymous aspects of individual autonomy with communal solidarity [and that] among these institutions are, above all, the family and religion." (113)

So it must be stressed that the quality of life possible in fully developed capitalisms is simply superior—for most people—to any quality of life possible before capitalism, or to any quality of life possible for most people as capitalism first developed/develops. There are scholars who argue the reverse—that the arrival of

Figure 5.1 Maslow's triangle

Source: Richard Tomkins (2003)

capitalism and of psychological depression went hand in hand—and there are many more (as we will note a little later) who feel that the stresses of modern capitalism explain much of the mental illness from which now so many suffer. (Ehrenreich, 2007) But even so, when we attempt to capture changes in the quality of life by using Maslow's hierarchy of human needs, we see that achieving all five levels of his pyramid (from basic physiological needs, through safety, belonging and love, and self-esteem—right through to self-actualization) is now, in fully developed capitalisms at least, a genuine possibility for most people in all social classes and in all genders.

The achievement of all five levels of the Maslow hierarchy is a real possibility, but that does not mean that it is a rock-solid certainty for everyone. Far from it: for capitalism's potential and capitalism's delivery are not identical. So although capitalism can (and is) legitimately praised by its advocates for delivering a better quality of life, and a higher level of personal freedom and self-development now than was available in the past, it can also be legitimately criticized by those who would reform it for failing to deliver as good a quality of life as it now has the potential to do. Those criticisms, as well as the plaudits, are worth our serious consideration, not least because they help illuminate the basic nature of the core challenges facing us as capitalism continues to develop.

Clearly, access to the full range of commodities, and to the associated space for individual development and autonomy, now emerging from capitalist economies is not the same for everyone. Inequalities of class and gender, as we have just seen, deny similar degrees of access to the full set of available life chances to the poor relative to the rich and to women relative to men; and inequalities of race and ethnicity (to which we will come in the next chapter)—some of which at least were in place long before capitalism arrived on the historical scene—continue to compound that difference of access in new and serious ways. But even when full access to the available range of goods and services is available to people, the relationship between their high levels of consumption and the quality of their lives remains more problematic than it may first appear. Not all consumption is necessary. Much of it these days is contrived—the product of heavy advertising and planned obsolescence. (Is an Apple iPhone 6 so much more potent than an Apple iPhone 5? Wasn't an Apple iPhone 5 once just the finest thing imaginable, so why now does it suddenly seem so inadequate? Has it changed, or have you?) Much of modern consumption is also subject to rapidly diminishing returns. (The first television entering the house may well transform leisure time, but the sixth television, the ninth . . . just how many televisions does anyone really need?) Moreover, so much of modern consumption, particularly in industries such as retailing, leisure activities and food production, is accessible to many of us simply because those producing it are paid so little. (We can afford to buy it because the people who provide it can't.) And so much of modern individualism comes with an associated psychic cost: it comes with a loss of a sense of community and purpose that, in less affluent times, helped protect individual workers and consumers from the tight vagaries of their condition.

So given that, it should come as no surprise that there is no perfect fit between levels of consumption and levels of happiness. Happiness seems to grow in line with consumption to a certain level, and then taper off. (Frey and Stutzer, 2002: 9) Beyond that level, as Peter Saunders put it,

> the more we get, the less satisfied we seem to be. In a world of bountiful commodities, we seem to be locked into a spiral of ever increasing accumulation as we seek to attain an always elusive sense of final contentment.
>
> (Saunders, 1995: 80)

Gregg Easterbrook called this mismatch between life getting better and people feeling worse "the progress paradox." (Easterbrook, 2003) Happiness would appear to decline as well, the more we move away from a managed toward an unmanaged capitalism, or (to say the same thing using the categories discussed in Chapter 2) from a coordinated market economy toward a liberal market one. Partly that may be because with freedom of choice necessarily comes the stress of choosing, so that the higher level of de-commodification associated with managed capitalisms can take at least some of that stress away. You only have to contrast the levels of insecurity about health care provision between health care consumers in a market-based system of the US kind (where fee-for-service provision is only partially covered by pre-paid health insurance) and patients in a national health service (with care free at the point of use) to see the difference. And partly the greater reported happiness of people in places such as Denmark and Finland might be the product of the way in which, in managed capitalisms, the character of work (rather than of consumption) tends to be more highly regulated. Work processes in all forms of advanced capitalism are less physically demanding than they were when industrial capitalism first began, but even so degrees of stress related to job insecurity, worker protection and the intensity of work do vary in different forms of capitalism.

Certainly, a capitalism based on full consumer rights and limited worker ones is not necessarily to be preferred to one in which the unbridled capacity to consume is constrained by greater protection for those providing the goods and services available for consumption. Americans on average may still enjoy a higher level of personal consumption than do most Western Europeans, for example, but they also put in a longer working week than is common in Western Europe—full-time American workers currently average 47 hours of labor per week, as against 36 in Sweden (Gallup, 2014; CNN, 2013)—and they certainly consume a far greater number of tranquilizers per head. This correlation between consumption, work and drugs may be coincidental rather than causal, but its existence does remind us that we all play many social roles. We are not just consumers; and individual happiness is the product of the whole person, not just of the consuming one. How else are we to explain "life satisfaction" scores that are as high in societies such as Ghana and Nigeria as they are in Ireland, the United Kingdom, Sweden and the United States? (Layard, 2005: 32–5)

In the end, however, how capitalism interacts with quality-of-life issues will not be settled by an appeal to facts and data alone, vital as that appeal is. Questions of conceptualization will also need to be addressed because here, as elsewhere in our discussion of capitalism and its effects, competing paradigms have different things to say. From a classically liberal perspective, what capitalism ultimately does is enhance individual freedom. Through the creation of labor and product markets, it leaves people free to sell their labor power wherever they choose, and it leaves them free to buy and sell things at their leisure. It also (as we will see next) comes to sustain political processes—democratic ones—that leave individual citizens free to choose or reject their government. Indeed, in a classic formulation of this general position by Milton Friedman, capitalist market processes are better guarantors of freedom even than democratic political ones, because when you buy and sell you see exactly what you are choosing and what you are leaving aside—your opportunity costs are clear—whereas a vote is at best a very blunt affair, able to choose only between broad political platforms and never clear on the long-term costs of any vote given or any vote withheld. (M. Friedman, 1976) And because the act of voting is of this kind, then for Friedman at least, there is a "line we dare not cross" as far as the size of government spending is concerned. Spend too much, and you disproportionately restrict the private market space within which people can be genuinely free.

But change your perspective, and things look a little different. That sense of "negative freedom"—freedom from government intervention and freedom from economic constraint—looks less adequate as a guide to the human condition once you bring into play the recognition of inherited inequalities over time. Once you begin to see that capitalist market competition produces losers as well as winners—and particularly when you begin to see that employees in a factory can lose their jobs if that factory fails, even though they themselves have done nothing but work hard for modest money—then the impact of capitalism on the quality of life needs some recalibration. To this sense of "negative freedom," social reformers have long added a demand for "positive freedoms": demands for the guarantee of a minimum set of social resources for each individual participating in the market place. Lyndon Johnson once explained that demand this way: "the man who is hungry," he said, "who cannot find work or educate his children, who is bowed by want, that man is not fully free." (Coates, 2011: 55) But give him access to high-quality education, to easily affordable health care and child support, to decent housing and to security from crime—then everyone's quality of life can rise together. A capitalism that does all that enhances human freedom. A capitalism that fails here does not.

CAPITALISM AND POLITICS

Classical liberal thinkers of Adam Smith's generation—and that includes men such as Thomas Jefferson—were not democrats in any modern sense of that term. They disliked autocratic rule and favored representative government. Indeed, some of them disliked autocratic rule to such a degree that they were prepared to take up arms against it; but even so, the representative form of government they sought was one based on only a limited franchise. They, and the generations of like-minded liberals that followed, spent a long time convinced that a full franchise would inevitably threaten the rights of private property they so valued, because so many of the people who would be voting under that franchise would not have any property or any interest in its preservation. This unease with the potential democratic threat to capitalist market processes has never entirely gone away, as is clear in the concerns of conservatives such as Milton Friedman with excessive government spending and regulation. But nonetheless and over time, anxieties about the contradiction between capitalism and democracy definitely eased, and the franchise was in fact steadily expanded. The democratic driver here was invariably popular pressure rather than capitalist logic: pressure initially from labor movements for a full male franchise, then pressure from a string of social movements for the extension of voting rights first to women, then to excluded ethnic minorities, and lately even to the very young. The result, eventually, has been the consolidation of a full franchise in most fully developed capitalisms: first in Australia at the turn of the twentieth century, and ultimately (after the civil rights protests of the 1960s) in the United States itself. Though voting rights still continue to be contested in the contemporary United States, it is clear that in general these days fully developed capitalisms and fully functioning democracies seem to go smoothly together.

But the relationship between capitalism and democracy was not always so cozy, and still today there is no automatic fit between economies organized on capitalist lines and political systems organized on democratic ones. As even as enthusiastic an advocate of capitalism as Peter Berger reluctantly recognized, "a useful way to describe the relationship between democracy and

Table 5.2 Year of establishment of democracy

Country	First attainment of democracy	Male democracy (if prior)	Reversal (excluding foreign occupation)	Beginning of present day democracy
Australia	(1903)			
Austria	1918		1934	1955
Belgium	1948	1919		
Canada	(1920)		(1931)	(1945)
Denmark	1915			
Finland	(1919)		1930	1944
France	1946	1884		
Germany	1919		1933 (1956)	1949 (1968)
Italy	1946	(1919)	[1922]	1946
Japan	1952			
Netherlands	1919	1917		
New Zealand	1907			
Norway	1915	1898		
Sweden	1918			
Switzerland	1971	c.1880	([1940])	([1944])
UK	1928	1918		
USA	c.1970			

Note: Brackets denotes qualifications, square brackets a process of reversal or re-establishment of male democracy. The qualifications include continued exclusion of voters by race/ethnicity and occasionally by political affiliation (communist).

Source: Therborn (1977: 11)

capitalism is to say that it is *asymmetrical.* Capitalism is a necessary—though not sufficient—condition for democracy but democracy is *not* a precondition for capitalism." (Berger, 1992: 11) As Berger among others is well aware, even for what are now advanced capitalisms, the routes to a full democratic franchise have varied. First-wave capitalisms with a strong middle class (such as the United Kingdom and United States) did incrementally extend the franchise in the sequence we have just described; but second-wave capitalisms (such as Germany and Japan) had a bumpier journey to the same end. Their contemporary democratic institutions were only finally established after a dark period of fascism in the German case and of military dominance of policy and politics in the Japanese one. It took a world war to cement democracy in these second-wave capitalisms. And among developing capitalisms, the routes to democracy have been different again: democratic institutions being established only after the casting off of colonial rule in the case of India; after the casting off of military dictatorships in a globally scattered string of cases that include Nigeria, Chile, Brazil and Argentina; and after the termination of long periods of communist rule (in Eastern Europe and in Russia itself).

The result has been that democracy in societies whose economies are organized on capitalist lines is best understood as coming, like capitalism itself, in *waves*; and best understood too as coming with *varying degrees of democratic depth and permanence*. There are definitely waves of democratic development in capitalist societies: a first wave in the nineteenth century that saw the franchise extended in most Western European countries and across the British Empire's "white dominions" (Goldblatt, 1997); a second wave after World War II that brought/brought back democracy to places such as West Germany, Japan, India, Italy and Greece; a third wave between 1974 and 1990 that brought democracy to a further thirty countries, mainly Catholic, starting in Portugal and Spain (Huntington, 1996: 3); and most recently a fourth wave extending democracy through parts of the former Soviet Union. By January 2000, indeed, Freedom House counted 120 countries as "democracies, the highest number and greatest percentage (62.5) in world history" and "a dramatic change even from 1990, when less than half the world's independent states were democracies." (Diamond, 2000: 412)

But waves do more than flow, of course. They also ebb. Democratic systems of government were replaced by more autocratic ones in Germany, Austria, Spain and ultimately even France in the years after 1933. Democracies fell to military coups in places as globally disparate as Greece, Brazil and Argentina in the 1960s. Ghana, Thailand, Sudan, Nigeria and Pakistan all slipped back (if in some cases only briefly) into military rule in the 1980s and 1990s. And most disturbing of all, democracies have "thinned"—in the sense of being drained of much of their content while retaining the formal trappings of elections and parties—in a whole range of countries of late. The fledgling

Russian democracy established after the fall of communism has certainly thinned under the presidencies of Vladimir Putin, and indeed many of what were once communist satellite states have definitely followed suit. Military regimes and personal dictatorships lack international legitimacy these days in ways they did not in the past—so even they now need the trappings of democratic political architecture—but behind any such democratic façade, many modern states actually combine capitalist forms of economic organization with highly authoritarian forms of political rule.

That should not necessarily surprise us, once we recognize that even in the recent histories of what are now core capitalist economies, we have no major example of full democratic institutions being established either before or in the early stages of capitalist industrial development. The degree of social dislocation and personal hardship associated with the transition *into* industrial capitalism is normally too severe to be compatible with a full franchise. Even in the British case, where in the Chartism of the 1830s and 1840s we see the first mass movement seeking a full franchise anywhere in an emerging capitalism, it was the defeat of that mass movement—not its success—that left the British state able to respond positively to the needs of an employing class determined to block trade unions, to keep wages low and to restrict factory regulation to the minimum. So it is entirely explicable, given that history, that in economies now in equivalent processes of transition—in economies newly industrializing on the periphery of the global capitalist system—democratic forms of politics should struggle to establish themselves or (where they do emerge) struggle to survive. Capitalism as a global system is characterized by "combined but uneven political development" as well as by "combined but even economic development." Indeed the one is in large measure the product of the other; so that we are now witnessing struggles for democratic reform in the conceptual "South" that mirror in important ways similar struggles, a century earlier, in the conceptual "North."

This complexity of the relationship between capitalism and democracy is no accident. It is the result of the way in which capitalism simultaneously releases forces and interests that reinforce the viability of democratic politics and forces and interests that challenge and undermine that viability. Capitalism certainly releases strong middle classes that ultimately acquire the self-confidence to demand representative forms of government answerable to their will. Capitalism also generates strong labor and social movements that are well-positioned to push middle-class-based representative government on to a full franchise: after all, if "all [men] are created equal . . ." the logic of the claim makes a full franchise hard to resist. But at the same time, the underlying and basic incompatibility of interests between the propertied and the propertyless that is endemic to capitalism always opens up the possibility that middle-class interests will be thought of as best served, in the short term at least, by an alliance of social classes that is anti-democratic. Recent history abounds with examples of this anti-democratic choice. To get the point, you only have to think of the alliance between the German middle class and Prussian militarism in pre-World War I Germany; or the alliance between the military and the middle class in Allende's Chile in the 1970s; or that between an emerging class of private entrepreneurs and established communist party officialdom in the contemporary Chinese one.

Even in core capitalisms, the propensity of unregulated capitalism to generate wealthy oligarchs as well as hard-pressed wage earners certainly gives the former the economic resources with which to buy excessive political influence (and so subvert democratic process) as and when they choose. That choice tends to be at its sharpest when rates of economic growth have stalled, or when levels of social deprivation have suddenly intensified. Arguably we are at such a moment now, which is why the question of the fit between capitalism and democracy is once more on our collective agenda in both the core and the periphery of the global capitalist system. In core capitalisms struggling with the problems of the modern welfare state, the key issue for democratic politics is whether an increasingly uneven distribution of income and wealth is draining the reality of popular control out of representative institutions. Is democracy in the North being increasingly "hollowed out," that is, by the embedding of powerful "democratic deficits"? In developing capitalisms, by contrast, the problem is otherwise. Can democracy survive there in countries in which it has already emerged, and emerge where it has yet to arrive? Will South America's "turn to the Left" in the last two decades produce a more managed capitalism, or simply a return to military rule; and will the Chinese Communist Party find a way of opening up China's political system to the democratic forces generated by its speedy industrialization, without either a repeat of Tiananmen Square or a collapse of the Chinese economy on a scale last seen in Russia after the fall of the Soviet Union?

These are big and difficult questions, but then we live in big and difficult times—times that demand of us a careful weighing of the strengths and weaknesses of different forms of capitalism, and a serious engagement with its key continuing legacies. That weighing and engagement awaits us now, in the final chapter of this brief introduction to the character and potential of capitalism.

FOR FURTHER EXPLORATION

To get your basic theoretical bearings here, start with Giddens (1971) and Walby (1991). Then read Lee & Turner (1996) and Devine (1997) on class; Esping-Andersen (2002) and Heymann & Earle (2010) on work and welfare; and Layard (2005) on happiness.

6

CAPITALISM AND ITS FUTURE

When looking forward rather than looking backward, one thing in particular is always missing: the empirical record of actual events. That is why projecting a thing such as capitalism forward in time requires a different sort of thought process and a different sort of evidence—not a reliance on hard data so much as a pursuit of theoretical understanding, not the accumulation of the record of things done so much as a sense of potential trajectories. But projections of capitalism and its future, if done well, are not arbitrary things: rather they grow in an organic fashion out of an understanding of how economies have worked in the past and how trends have built up in the present. We have seen already that from its inception capitalism demonstrated a capacity for both growth and recession, plus more recently, in its core areas at least, a capacity to combine general affluence with the persistence of significant inequalities in income and wealth. We have seen capitalism emerge out of, and ultimately obliterate, other ways of organizing economic life, while at the same time sustaining in modified forms older patterns of life and thought; and we have seen capitalism generate a new morality based on market values that ultimately sits in tension with moralities based on pre-capitalist institutions and modes of being. It is now time to pull together all this ebb and flow of capitalism and its context, in a final conversation about economic growth and its problems, about inequality and its consequences, about markets and their limits, and about the clash of the old and the new in a world full of production and trade.

THE PROBLEM OF GROWTH

You don't have to be a Marxist to recognize that, since the financial crisis of 2008, public policy in advanced capitalist economies has struggled to reconstitute patterns of economic growth strong enough to sustain full employment and rising living standards for all. Nor do you have to be a radical to see that some of the basic tensions endemic to capitalist economies now dominate life in many societies beyond the advanced capitalist core. Even the dramatic expansion of the Chinese economy—the single most striking feature of global capitalism in the first decades of the new millennium—has come at a considerable internal price for the generations of Chinese workers and entrepreneurs caught up inside it: including problems of environmental pollution (to which we will come), problems of income inequality (of a kind we have already seen in core capitalisms) and problems of agrarian dislocation and industrial work intensity (of a kind common to those advanced capitalisms in their early stages of development). (Piovani and Li, 2011) The inter-connected nature of developed and developing capitalisms in our highly globalized world means that these problems in core and developing economies are both linked and shared. The level of wages and the conditions of work prevalent in developing economies impose a downward pressure on remuneration, and an upward pressure on the length and intensity of work, in more developed economies; while the adverse effects on global levels of demand released by those pressures make it progressively harder over time for developing economies to sustain the growth rates and employment potentials of their own industries without generating internal markets for the goods they now export to more advanced economies abroad.

While total levels of demand for both consumption and investment goods were growing in the core capitalist economies—as they most definitely were in the two decades prior to the 2008 financial crisis—these underlying problems could be held at bay, but even then only with certain long-term costs. As we initially saw in Chapter 2, the first of those costs was the growing fragility of that total level of demand over time, as the capacity of consumers in both the United States and the United Kingdom came increasingly to rest on the running up of personal debt and the exploitation of inflated house prices, rather than on rising wages. The second was the generation of ever larger trade imbalances between successful export economies (including advanced ones such as Germany and Japan, and not just China) and less successful ones (primarily in this instance the United States and the United Kingdom, where the credit bubble was at its greatest). These rising levels of both consumer debt and foreign debt helped sustain capitalist growth across the entire global system for nearly twenty years—a period now often labeled "The Great Moderation"—but debt, of course, is a dangerous and highly fragile basis for any successful long-term period of growth. For debt ultimately rests on confidence—the confidence of both borrowers and lenders that debts can be repaid by earnings yet to come—and that confidence is a fickle mistress, easily built up and equally easily lost.

It was easily built up as US and UK house prices soared in the years either side of the millennium. It was equally easily lost when the excessive use of subprime mortgages that had sustained the housing boom began to trigger high levels of debt default and falling house prices in both economies by 2006 and 2007. (Coates & Dickstein, 2011) So when the credit bubble finally broke in the United States—when for that terrifying moment in September 2008 the entire global credit system dominated by Wall Street banks suddenly stalled, with no single financial institution able to be sure that any other major financial institution was actually solvent—confidence drained out of the entire global system, releasing a downward spiral of business closures and worker lay-offs in 2008–9 (and a subsequent Eurozone crisis) from which the global economy as a whole was still only slowly recovering half a decade later. For confidence lost on that scale and with that degree of abruptness is not a confidence that is easily restored: which is why even in 2015, as this final chapter is drafted, policy-makers in advanced capitalist economies continue to struggle with low rates of economic growth and high rates of job insecurity—rates that make governments electorally unpopular wherever they occur. And they are struggling with these immediate issues of low economic growth and high unemployment in the context of a longer-term trend, evident in the trajectories of all "richly highly industrialized—or better, increasingly deindustrialized—capitalist countries" of a "persistent decline in the rate of economic growth." (Streeck, 2014) Average annual rates of economic growth for the top twenty OECD countries in the early 1970s exceeded 4 percent. It currently hovers around 2 percent.

It is now clear that a return to sustained economic growth in core capitalist economies requires two things that are extraordinarily difficult both to generate and to put together. One is a balance of demand and supply—a new social settlement—that can recreate confidence in investors that (after they buy new equipment and employ more people) they will indeed be able to sell a sufficient quantity of goods to generate the profits necessary to sustain yet more investment: how to break out, that is, of what Lawrence Summers and others have called the problem of "secular stagnation." (Summers, 2013, 2014). The other is how to find the next technological fix that can stimulate a significant rise in the productivity of labor. For as we first saw in Chapter 2, only if those in employment generate a greater output per hour year after year can general living standards continue to rise; because if they do not, general living standards can rise only by extending the length of the working day and the intensity of the work process (and there are physical limits to that), and particular living standards can rise only by pushing down the living standards of others. As we saw earlier, general living standards rose in core capitalist economies in the years immediately after World War II (roughly 1948–73) by shifting employment from low-productivity agriculture into higher-productivity manufacturing, and by increasing productivity there by introducing semi-automated production systems (Fordism). General living standards rose from the late 1980s in advanced economies with, by then, large service sectors only by applying the new computer technology across each economy as a whole (including in service industries such as retailing) and by workers extending their hours, their intensity of work and their levels of personal debt. The task before us now is to find a new productivity booster at a moment when the scale of hours worked and debt accumulated have both maxed out, and when every economic sector that can be computerized has been.

Sadly, it is at least worth facing the possibility that such a new boost in labor productivity may be slow in coming, or may never come at all. In a stimulating and subsequently much discussed academic paper published in 2012, the respected American economic historian Robert J. Gordon floated just such a possibility: of only a 0.2 percent annual increase in real per capita disposable income for the bottom 99 percent of the US income distribution over the next 25–40 years because of "faltering innovation and the six headwinds"—headwinds he listed as an aging population, rising inequality, factor price equalization, educational underperformance, environmental regulations and the tax and debt burden. (R. Gordon, 2012, 2014) The Gordon argument was US specific, and explicitly did not exclude rapid "catch-up" growth elsewhere in the global system; but it pointed to the difficulty of continually raising living standards at a post-World War II rate without another round of "great inventions" of the kind which (after 1890) had ultimately made the growth story of the second half of the twentieth century possible. Gordon wrote of three "industrial revolutions" in the past: the first built on coal, steam and railways before 1830; the second built on electricity, the internal combustion engine and chemicals after 1890; and the third built on computers, the web and mobile phones since 1960. Each industrial revolution had initially sparked significant rises in labor productivity, but the impact of the third was significantly less marked and prolonged than that of the second; and anyway, all three are now spent. Without a fourth "industrial revolution," where do we go, except into a period of very low income growth?

This is somber stuff, but genuinely worth thinking about, for two reasons at least. One is that if a boost in labor productivity continues to escape us, those of us currently privileged enough to live in advanced capitalisms will have to adjust our thinking about our future in a deep and profound way. Since 1945, we have all tended to assume that sustained economic growth is a genuine possibility, that improved living standards are our general and legitimate expectation, and that politicians and political programs are properly to be judged by their relationship to the speed (but not the direction, always upward) of this trajectory. But if labor productivity is flat, so too must be general living standards; and if that flatness persists then politics will become, even more than it is today, a zero-sum game about income distribution rather than income growth. Fights about wealth for some at the expense of poverty for others is never an easy or a pleasant politics.

Which takes us to the other reason for reflection here. Advanced capitalisms already possess vast architectures of income redistribution. We call them welfare states—structures redistributing the products of our collective labor between the various social groups who need access to them: redistributing claims on resources between children, working adults and the retired; between the healthy and the sick; and between those in paid labor and those excluded from paid labor by function (childbearing or the care of the infirm), disability or involuntary unemployment. When rates of economic growth are strong and labor productivity is high, the basic "pay-as-you-go" principle underpinning welfare provision works fine. People in paid work support those out of work by transfers of income through taxation. But when economic growth stalls and labor productivity dips, that transfer becomes necessarily contentious. It is contentious now: not least between baby boomers poised to enjoy generous pensions and health care and a younger generation supporting that generosity while being themselves strapped for money, for secure employment and for adequate pension prospects down the line. The contemporary "crisis of the welfare state" of which we now hear so much is anchored ultimately in the stalled growth rates of the advanced sections of the global economy. (Pierson, 2001) For the sake of generational peace, therefore, as well as for the sake of rising private affluence, our big need now is to find as quickly as we can an effective route back to strong and sustained rates of economic growth.

THE PROBLEM OF INEQUALITY

Something else worth thinking about that is also rather somber is the current state of income and wealth inequality within and between capitalist economies. Income and wealth inequality between fully developed and newly developing capitalisms has always been stark, as we saw in Chapter 5. It has also been historically persistent and entrenched. For all the claims of neo-classical economists about market forces inevitably equalizing returns to factors of production (including labor) over time, we saw then that although average incomes were higher in most economies in 1980 than they had been in 1900, the *gap* in average incomes between the economies of the North and the economies of the South had not declined commensurately. Fortunately the scale and persistence of that gap is clearly diminishing now, as economies such as China and Kenya at long last begin to raise their average incomes to levels that qualify them—in WTO terms— as "middle-income economies." Indeed and because they are, as a leading World Bank report recently put it, it seems likely that

> the period between the fall of the Berlin Wall and the Great Recession saw probably the most profound reshuffle of individual incomes on the global scale since the Industrial Revolution. This was driven by high growth rates of populous and formerly poor or very poor countries like China, Indonesia and India; and on the other hand, by the stagnation or decline of incomes in sub-Saharan Africa and post-communist countries as well as among poorer segments of the populations of rich countries.
> (Lakner & Milanovic, 2014)

But note the key term there—reshuffle—and the dating—after 1989. Both remind us that, in relation to global income distribution at least, the main story for the second half of the twentieth century was *not* one of generalized equalization of incomes, however desirable that might have been. It was rather one of modest improvements, unevenly distributed. As we saw earlier, after 1945 average income levels rose significantly only in a limited number of fully developed core capitalist economies, in the process leaving elsewhere literally billions of people locked in debilitating levels of absolute poverty—struggling to survive on miserably low wages: as late as 2010, "almost one in three workers worldwide living on under US$2 a day." (Selwyn, 2014: 2) So even today, as the CEOs of Unilever and Rothschild recently jointly reported,

> despite recent emerging-market growth, the world economy [remains] a place of staggering extremes. The 1.2 billion poorest people on the planet account for just 1 percent of global consumption, while the billion richest are responsible for 72 percent. . . . The 85 richest people in the world have accumulated the same wealth as the bottom 3.5 billion [while] one in eight people go to bed hungry every night.
>
> (de Rothschild & Polman, 2014)

In relation to this same issue—the global distribution of income—the main story of the opening decades of the new millennium is, if anything, more disturbing still. It is that, within both fully developed and developing capitalisms, income and wealth inequality is widening again. It is widening within developing economies: according to the UNDP 2013 report on *Humanity Divided*, "On average—and taking into account population size—income inequality increased by 11 percent in developing countries between 1990 and 2010." (UNDP, 2013) This, in the context of a growing recognition, in the literature on economic growth, that—far from the old orthodoxy that had countries needing to choose between equality and efficiency (Okun, 1975)—"reduced inequality and sustained growth may be two sides of the same coin" and that "sustainable economic reform is possible only if its benefits are widely shared." (Berg & Ostry, 2011: 15). The OECD recently put it this way, in their report on UK economic performance: "income inequality has a sizeable and statistically negative impact on growth and redistributive policies achieving greater equality in disposable income have no adverse growth consequences." (Cingano, 2014: 6)

For growing income inequality is not just a problem in the developing world. As the OECD report on the United Kingdom makes clear, inequality is becoming a potential barrier to growth in core capitalisms as well. Certainly, levels of income inequality in some core capitalist economies—not least the US economy—have recently returned to a pitch last seen in the years immediately before World War I. This intensified scale of inequality is currently not only dividing the life chances open to members of one social class from those open to members of less privileged classes. It is also dividing the life chances open to members of different generations even within the same social class. We will comment later on the relationship between shrinking generational options and the emergence of Islamic fundamentalism in vast areas of the Middle East. But for the moment it is enough to note that the intensification of global competition after the fall of the Soviet Union and the tightening of economic conditions after the 2008 financial crisis have combined to open up a significant gap in life chances, in the core capitalisms themselves, between generations of even the hitherto highly successful middle class. Intensified competition and sharp recession together robbing the grandchildren of successful baby boomers of the adequate starting salaries, high levels of job security and generous pension programs enjoyed by many of those fortunate enough to have entered the paid labor force between the end of World War II and the first oil crisis of the 1970s. (Little, 2014)

If the data recently gathered by the French economic historian Thomas Piketty is an accurate guide, this steady increase in various kinds of material and social inequality may distress some of us (as it certainly does him) but it should not surprise any of us. For if he is right, the dominant tendency in a capitalist economy is for inequalities of particularly wealth ownership to grow incrementally over time. Such pessimism about the future of income and wealth distribution under capitalism was not normal in the boom years of the 1950s and 1960s, when the conventional wisdom in governing economic circles was that inequality everywhere could "be expected to follow a 'bell curve.' In other words, it should first increase and then decrease over the course of industrialization and economic development." (Piketty, 2014: 13) But the Piketty thesis challenges that optimism in a powerful and convincing way, arguing that

> when the rate of return on capital exceeds the rate of growth of output and income, as it did in the nineteenth century and seems quite likely to do again in the twenty-first . . . then it logically follows that inherited wealth grows faster than output and income. People with inherited wealth need save only a portion of their income from capital to see that capital grow more quickly than the economy as a whole. Under such conditions, it is almost inevitable that inherited wealth will dominate wealth amassed from a lifetime's labor by a wide margin.
>
> (26)

So if the Piketty thesis is right, we face a future—unless we act now—in which "wealth is not only distributed more unevenly than income," but also one in which more of that wealth "is clearly unearned." (Segal, 2014)

The Piketty thesis is not without its critics—critics from the Right questioning the reliability of his data and the accuracy of his mathematics, and critics from the Left reminding us that income inequality declined for three decades after World War II when labor movements were strong and progressive taxation broadly popular. But his work does underscore the degree to which, even in advanced capitalisms, access to both material resources and to political power tends to become less equal over time unless public policy intervenes to slow down the trend. (Piketty's policy of choice is one he admits is probably utopian, namely a global tax on capital.) One question to ask ourselves, therefore, as we try to go forward, is whether contemporary levels of inequality are actually taking us back: back, as Thomas Piketty fears that they are, toward the "patrimonial capitalism" of the nineteenth century; back toward that period of early capitalism (America's "Gilded Age" or France's "La Belle Époque") in which both economic and political power in ostensibly democratic capitalisms was dominated by inherited wealth? The other question to ask ourselves, as we reflect upon this data, is that if we are drifting toward such an oligarchy, does the drift actually matter?

THE PROBLEM OF MARKET-BASED INEQUALITIES

Many progressives, including Thomas Piketty himself, think that it does matter; and that it matters primarily because of the many undesirable consequences associated with income and wealth inequalities of the contemporary scale. (Wilkinson & Pickett, 2009) That full range is more than we can deal with here; and for our purposes, it is perhaps enough to explore the impact of large inequalities of wealth and income on three of the dimensions of a functioning capitalism with which we have been centrally concerned: on levels of demand, on the proper role of markets, and on the particular social needs of markets in which people sell their labor power.

Large inequalities of income and wealth do make it disproportionately difficult, in the short and medium term, to regenerate
significant rates of economic growth and job creation by the
stimulation of consumer demand. That really matters because consumer demand is still the main driver of growth and employment
in advanced capitalisms—responsible, for example, for at least 70
percent of that growth in the US economy—and because it is,
inequality on any large scale simply doesn't help policy-makers
trying to kick-start a stagnant economy. There is only so much
demand that, say, the privileged 1 percent can bring to the market
place. This shortfall in purchasing power was particularly visible
as a problem in the post-Great Recession US economy, where
(by 2013) the top 3 percent of income earners were receiving
30.5 percent of total incomes and the next 7 percent an additional
16.8 percent—so leaving just half of national income for the
remaining 90 percent of the US population. As the *Financial Times*'
Martin Wolf observed at the time, this skewed and highly unequal
distribution of income had both immediate and long-term
negative effects. Immediately, as we have just noted, it weakened
demand and slowed down business investment because that
demand was missing. In the longer term, it eroded the general
quality of so vital a thing as the US education system, so helping
undermine the future competitiveness of US-made goods and
services in both foreign and domestic markets. Such an excessive
level of inequality, as he put it, "is such a drag on economies"
(Wolf, 2014) that anyone interested in the long-term success of
capitalism, and the long-term prosperity of people living in
economies organized on capitalist lines, needs in his view to be
thinking of ways to bring the distribution of income and wealth
back into some more balanced condition.

Moreover, if income and wealth inequality reaches the scale
to which Piketty has drawn our attention, it does more than
simply block off immediate levels of consumer demand. It also
helps undermine one of the central claims made for unregulated
capitalist markets by economists keen to minimize government
involvement in them: namely that over time unregulated product
and labor markets generate the most optimal distribution of
resources possible, and so should be left alone to do so. Now,
most everyone can agree that unregulated capitalist markets would

be capable of achieving this optimality if each consumer within them had the same purchasing power. Then markets would allocate resources in ways sensitive to the intensity, as well as to the volume, of consumer preferences in a manner that no centrally planned economy could ever hope to match. But with incomes and wealth so skewed in favor of a privileged few, as they are globally and nationally now, the intensity and volume of preferences of the very rich necessarily take precedence over the intensity and volume of preferences of the less fortunate, unless markets are regulated in some fashion. And even if markets do ever begin on a level playing field of incomes, their internal competitive dynamic must steadily and inevitably undermine that equality as winners move ahead and losers fall behind. Unregulated markets in capitalist economies are great mechanisms for the generation of *inequalities* between individuals; and the inequalities they generate are invariably cumulative. Unregulated markets and deepening socio-economic differences, in that sense, go together. In general the children of the poor stay poor; and because they do, at the very least, those who would leave markets unregulated have to explain how they square their passion for individual freedom and equality with the inequality and differences in social empowerment that divide the children of the rich from the children of the poor. Some degree of income and wealth inequality is clearly functional to capitalism—acting as an incentive for innovation, risk taking and hard work—but when levels of inequality become too acute, the general legitimacy of the system as a whole comes into question in the minds of more and more people. Arguably, that general questioning of the legitimacy of only lightly regulated capitalism was exactly what happened briefly in the wake of the financial crisis of 2008. (Plender, 2012)

Piketty-like levels of income and wealth inequality do one other thing too that we need to bear in mind when reflecting on the strengths and weaknesses of capitalism and its markets. They undermine any notion that capitalist labor markets automatically generate "a fair day's work for a fair day's pay," or that there is so close a relationship (and so perfect a fit) between the social value of work done and the wages/salaries which that work attracts that an unregulated capitalist wage system has moral force as well as market logic. It was never the case, even in early capitalism, that the jobs with the greatest social value earned the highest incomes; and for all the pressure of trade unions and social reformers over many decades, it is still not the case today. The highest salaries currently paid in LMEs of the US and UK variety go to bankers. Indeed, bank bonuses were momentarily a matter of public outrage in the immediate aftermath of the 2008 financial crisis, when it became more generally known than hitherto that senior salaries in the US financial industry were running 70 percent higher than those elsewhere in the economy. This in a financial sector much of whose work was recently described by the UK's chief financial regulator as "socially useless activity" (Cassidy, 2010)—just speculation with other people's money—and in a sector so poorly regulated that this excessive speculation brought it crashing down. The people doing the key jobs that we all need done are never the highest-paid members of a capitalist labor force. The nurses who tend us when we are sick; the first responders who charge into personal danger when we are caught up in house fires or school shootings; the men and women who run the sewage systems, the electricity grid, the reservoirs and water systems on which life actually depends—none of these people are very highly paid. But over time, we all sort of come to accept this subtle but hidden labor market injustice. It comes to seem natural even though it is not; and we are only jolted into a recognition of this on-going gap between social worth and personal reward when a major economic crisis occurs, or when a new body of research data (such as that produced by Thomas Piketty and his colleagues) throws strong light into dark places. We have been jolted by both lately—to our general advantage, I think—in ways that leave at least two huge sets of questions worthy of at least a preliminary kind of answer.

The first set of questions is this. Are there any things that should *not* be allocated, even in economies successfully organized on capitalist lines, by standard market processes? (Satz, 2012; Sandel, 2012; Skidelsky & Skidelsky, 2013) Are there things too complex for private enterprise to provide and for markets to allocate—public goods that the state should provide free at the point of use; and are there things that private enterprise could provide and markets could allocate that are simply too undesirable for civilized societies to allow to be distributed in that fashion? (Sandel, 2012)

And can things that are "cheap" actually be provided at too a high a price: too high, that is, in terms of the underpayment of those who provide them? (Shell, 2009) Are there, in other words, technical and moral limits to markets? On the technical limits, even Adam Smith thought that national defense, justice and education were all public goods that private sector provision could not allocate adequately and fairly, and you may have others to add to his list. Many British people, for example, long used to health care free at the point of use inside the National Health Service, might add health care. I certainly would. And where do you stand on the exploitation of child labor or on the morality of selling body parts or on allowing a free market in pornography and prostitution; let alone where do you stand on the morality of the slave trade that was so vital to the early accumulation of capital in both the United Kingdom and the United States? Should people be able to buy people, or does capitalism work best when set inside strict boundaries created by moral codes that pre-date and transcend it?

That last question then takes us to a second cluster of issues worthy of careful consideration when thinking about the limits of markets: issues around the appropriateness of different kinds of regulation in different kinds of markets. All capitalist markets need a basic level of regulation: on property rights, weights and measures, coinage and the like. That is not generally in dispute, and indeed even markets for items as inanimate as baked beans are widely recognized as requiring further regulation. The regulation of food standards was quite properly recognized early in the nineteenth century as a key requirement for the effective functioning of a safe capitalist market. The extra questions here relate not to markets in which people buy the things they need, but to markets in which they sell their own labor in return for wages. The extra questions relate to animate rather than inanimate markets. Do those markets require extra and unique forms of regulation and, if so, what kind? Is it all right for people to be left unemployed if a factory closes, just as cans of baked beans are left on the store shelves if demand for them suddenly falls? Or are people different from baked beans? It is hardly the beans' fault that they remain unsold, just as it is rarely the workers' fault that the factory closes—but it closes anyway. Inside the unsold cans, beans last (at least for a while); but can people last (even for a short period) without an adequate flow of funds? And if they cannot, are the people fortunate enough to retain employment then under some moral obligation to help out those less fortunate in the job market than themselves?

In other words, what exactly should the relationship be between personal responsibility, private charity and state-provided welfare support in economies subject to periodic waves of large-scale involuntary unemployment? And inside labor markets, should there be limits set, by governments elected by the people who participate in or depend upon those markets, on the minimum and/or maximum wages and salaries to be paid to any one individual for the sale of his/her labor power? Or should labor markets be simply allowed to function like any other commodity market, without external price setting of any kind, and should the rest of us then live easy with whatever outcomes those unregulated labor markets generate? Modern political parties often divide on just these issues, which makes it all the more important that we all come to our own carefully considered view of each and every one of them.

THE PROBLEM OF PRE-EXISTING CONDITIONS

But not all the issues before us in modern elections, and not all the social and political problems with which we are currently beset, can be so directly traced to the character and working of capitalist markets. In many ways, life would be so much easier if they could. But they can't. They can't even though in that earlier classic debate between Marx and Weber on capitalism and its potential, as we saw earlier, the Marxist side of the debate expected capitalism to do just that: to be so all-consuming an experience as to literally drown out and destroy every other (pre-capitalist) form of social definition and understanding. Capitalism was supposed to be entirely self-unmasking, Marx and Engels wrote in *The Communist Manifesto*, because of the ruthless egotism it encourages and the erosion of religious beliefs that it triggers. As they put it:

> The bourgeoisie, wherever it has got the upper hand, has put an end to all feudal, patriarchal, idyllic relations. It has pitilessly torn asunder the

motley feudal ties that bound man to his "natural superiors", and has left remaining no other nexus between man and man than naked self-interest, than callous "cash payment" ... In one word, for exploitation veiled by religious and political illusions, it has substituted naked, shameless, direct, brutal exploitation.

(Marx & Engels, 1848: 37–8)

But Max Weber, for one, was not so sure. He was aware of the awfulness of industrial life, and the appalling conditions of Victorian proletarian labor; but he expected those to ease over time, and to co-exist with social differences based on long-established dimensions of status rather than on newly created divisions of class. In all that, he was surely right; and we still live today in societies in which pre-existing sets of social relationships and bodies of intellectual understanding co-exist with capitalism, its new classes and its new science—the new and the old each reinforced by the relationship with the other. The result is some of the most intractable social divisions, and associated social problems, that we currently face.

RACE AND ETHNICITY

The most obvious one, in advanced capitalisms, is the persistence of social divisions and social tensions based on race and ethnicity. Capitalism did not invent those tensions, but nor did it rub them out. Instead, the resetting of economic life on capitalist lines reinforced and intensified racial and ethnic divisions, the latter of which at least had long been in play. It remains an open question whether racial tensions based on skin color were a major source of social tension prior to capitalism—most people lived, worked and died, after all, in very restricted societies that few strangers entered—but it is clearly the case that once substantial capital accumulation had begun in predominantly "white" societies, that tension emerged quickly and remained potent thereafter. That was in part because in the early stages of capitalist industrialization, much of the capital being deployed came from commodities produced by slave labor and the profits made by trading in slaves. The bulk of those slaves were African: writing into the very core of the thought processes of both early capitalists and early industrial workers—particularly in the United States—a black–white division that has never gone away.

There have been moments in the history of capitalism when white workers and non-white workers have stood together in common opposition to unacceptable levels of exploitation by the private owners of capital, but more normally white workers have seen their black/brown equivalents as a threat to their own meager hold on the basic necessities of life, and have resisted them accordingly. Private employers have been perfectly willing, in all but a tiny minority of cases, to reinforce this division by paying non-white workers less than white workers and by denying them equivalent levels of status and promotion, so producing a labor force that—both in the past and now—is heavily stratified by socially constructed racial categories. Race is not the only form of stratification running through capitalist labor forces. We have noted gender stratification already, and we will note national divisions soon. Nor was it (or is it) a form of stratification that prevents the emergence of a black/brown middle class. But it is a persistent and on-going form of stratification in capitalist economies and their associated societies: in both we see the articulation of a capitalist-induced class system with a capitalist-enhanced racial one that produces a complex layering of experience and interest.

The sense of white racial superiority reflected in such a pattern of social structuration received an enormous boost at the end of the nineteenth century, when the combined but uneven development of emerging industrial capitalisms triggered a "rush to empire": the forced colonization of much of Africa, the forced opening of Chinese markets to European and American goods, and (after 1918) the forced creation of new states in a Middle East subject to European oversight. The expansion of colonial empires controlled by the more developed capitalisms of Western Europe fueled a white racism already present in the older empires of Portugal and Spain; and as a string of new industrializing nation-states (such as Germany and Italy) rushed after 1870 to catch up with earlier industrializers and colonial powers (such as the United Kingdom and France), a newly intensified sense of nationalism and a deepening racism fused into a generalized belief in the superiority of "northern" cultures that remains potent in popular consciousness in core capitalisms even today.

That same late nineteenth-century "rush to empire" also fueled a parallel rush to war, as ruling groups in rapidly emerging industrial capitalisms built powerful military-industrial complexes that they eventually used upon each other. The nineteenth-century organization of industrial capitalist economies inside national units, and the resulting competition between those national units, reinforced tensions (and twice in the twentieth century triggered global warfare) across ethnic and national boundaries that had previously been played out militarily only by armies equipped with pre-capitalist military technologies. Capitalism, as it developed, gave those armies some seriously dangerous toys with which to play, including by the end weapons of mass destruction of such a scale as to threaten the viability of the planet itself; so that for a period at least (roughly the century from 1850 to 1950) capitalist industrialization, inter-imperialist rivalries and rampant militarism all grew together.

The second of those global conflicts was so awful, however, and so mutually destructive of life, property and already meager living standards that it ultimately persuaded many European ruling groups to merge their economies into first a trading, then an economic and ultimately a political union, so removing one major source of military tension between capitalist powers. But both world wars were scarred, not simply by horrendous casualty figures and (in the second one) by appalling crimes against civilian populations, particularly against women. Both were also scarred by deliberate, racially inspired genocides—of the Armenians by the Turks in 1915 and of European Jewry by the Germans after 1941—and both left intact global economic inequalities that kept older if less lethal ethnic tensions alive, well and flourishing. We noted earlier the post-World War II patterns of labor migration. Those migrations not only fueled economic growth in the core capitalisms. They also reignited in those capitalisms powerful, long-rooted and often unspoken ethnic tensions—tensions between indigenous labor forces and new arrivals that bubbled under the surface of social and political life so long as the core economies expanded, but then reappeared in all their ugliness whenever that economic growth stalled.

RELIGION

So, Karl Marx notwithstanding, capitalism did not rub out either race or ethnicity as powerful sources of self-definition and social division. Oh that it had. Sadly and on the contrary, it ultimately amplified both; and it has so far proved equally impotent in the face of religions and the well-established pre-capitalist tendency to fight ferocious religious wars. Marx and Weber both expected extensive secularization to come with full capitalism, and indeed Western Europe saw a lot of just that secularization as capitalism developed. But religion remained (and remains) important as a reinforcing source of self-definition in the many ethnic communities that collectively make up the US population; and religious ways of understanding the world remained largely unchallenged in the many societies only peripherally touched by capitalism. And religion came bouncing back—big time—in a more fundamentalist form in both core and peripheral capitalisms as capitalist prosperity faltered from the 1970s. Capitalism did not create religious fundamentalism, but the spread and performance of capitalism in the last five decades is certainly one key factor helping to explain the depth and severity of the confrontation between (and within) major religions on the global stage today.

Ironically, part of the reason for the resurgence of religion as a source of political division in the modern world was capitalism's very success in out-confronting Soviet Communism. When the Berlin Wall fell in 1989, there were many celebratory intellectuals willing to assert *The End of History* and to claim that the age of competing secular ideologies was now a thing of the past. (Fukuyama, 1992) But with the fall of the Soviet Union in 1991, history did not so much end as re-assert itself culturally in a pre-capitalist form. The severity of the communist suppression of religion in both the Eastern European and North Asian parts of its empire after 1945 had the paradoxical consequence of helping to keep those religions alive, strengthening them by linking them to sentiments (and occasionally, as in Poland after 1970, movements) of resistance to Soviet imperial rule. Take that rule away, and religious sentiment flourished in its newfound freedom: it flourished as Catholicism in Eastern Europe, as Greek Orthodoxy in Russia itself, and as Islam in Northern Asia. Indeed, and even more paradoxically, the leading capitalist power—the United States—played its own role in keeping a particularly fundamentalist brand of Islam alive through the late Soviet period: by sustaining the Saudi Arabian government (a key funder of extreme Islam) as a stabilizing force in the Middle East, by supporting a tyrannical modernizing regime in Iran after 1953 that was ultimately overthrown by a theocratic revolution in 1979, and by funding through the 1980s the Islamic-inspired mujahedeen (including Osama bin Laden) fighting to liberate Afghanistan from Soviet occupation.

That support might have mattered less for the future stability of global politics had it not also coincided with a second development, linked less to imperialism than to that other tendency apparently endemic to global capitalism: the tendency for combined but uneven economic development. By the late 1970s the countries of the Middle East had long thrown off the formal shackles of Western colonialism, but their economies still remained locked into a subordinate position in the prevailing international division of labor—unable (except for Israel) to break through to sustained growth and rising living standards for the bulk of their populations. (As late as 2006, for example, the ILO was reporting that the Middle East and North Africa had the highest rates of unemployment in the world—at 13.2 percent, higher even than sub-Saharan Africa. (T. Friedman, 2006)) It was not that their first generations of post-colonial Arab governments did not seek sustained economic growth. They certainly did, turning either to the United States or to the Soviet Union for both guidance and support. It was rather that in that pursuit they expanded their higher education systems significantly, in the process calling into existence a generation of highly trained young adults who graduated into a world that still offered them only limited opportunities for economic and social advancement. The first modernizing Arab governments of the post-colonial period were largely secular ones. They were also often dictatorial. In resistance to both their secularity and their brutality, as well as to their economic failure and political corruption, key areas of the Middle East saw a turn after 1970 to a more fundamentalist form of Islamic opposition. It was a turn made by sections of a generation who were disaffected with Western-style capitalism (and actively hostile to the state of Israel as its regional embodiment) while also being equipped with capitalist skills. Osama bin Laden was the most famous (or notorious) of these converts to a fundamentalist Islam, but he was by no means the only one.

Add this final element to the pot, and the resurgence of fundamentalist religions in an increasingly capitalist world makes a crazy kind of sense. Within the core capitalisms of the global system, and particularly within the United States itself, pockets of resistance remained throughout the post-war years to the materialism associated with capitalist affluence, and to the assertiveness of social movements (of ethnic minorities and an entire gender) seeking to spread that affluence more widely. Some of that resistance remained determinedly secular: taking the form of right-wing populist movements opposed to immigration, to trade unions, even—as with libertarians in the United States—to the expansion of the role of the democratic state itself. But some was equally determinedly religious. Christianity—particularly Protestant Christianity—saw its own turn to fundamentalism as the twentieth century closed: a fundamentalism that manifested itself in opposition both to a progressive social agenda (on things such as abortion and gay marriage) and to jihadist Islam (not least through its enthusiasm for the traditional claims of fundamentalist Judaism within the state of Israel). Secular capitalism defeated secular communism in the Cold War that had structured international politics for nearly half a century after the end of World War II, but in that defeat a victorious capitalism inadvertently left the global stage open to a clash of religious fundamentalisms more reminiscent of international politics in the immediate pre-capitalist period.

All of which leaves us with the on-going issue of the relationship between capitalism and non-capitalist forms of identity and politics. Where capitalism has raised general living standards, the tensions between the social classes it created, and between the social groups it inherited from the past, have normally softened. Prosperous people rarely feel the need to physically challenge the prosperity of others. Fully developed capitalisms these days rarely fight each other. But thus far, capitalism has only generated prosperity unevenly, and to some degree at least capitalism has generated prosperity for some only by denying it to others. And in any event, even where capitalism has been particularly successful in raising living standards, currently that success is itself increasingly difficult to replicate. So the question we have to ask ourselves is what role, if any, can we (as educated individuals) play in helping to bring into existence a world in which prosperity is both raised and more equally shared, and a world in which people embrace and celebrate their differences (of gender, sexual orientation, race, ethnicity, language, culture and religion) rather than discriminate against or fight each other because of them. It is one of the greatest challenges of the modern age.

THE PROBLEM OF THE COMMONS

The other great challenge facing members of advanced capitalist societies is this. How to do any of this global economic recon-struction without so adversely impacting the natural environment that economic growth itself becomes impossible, or becomes possible in one generation only by denying the possibility of it to generations yet to come?

This is genuinely a new problem. As John Urry recently noted, "almost all forms of nineteenth- and twentieth-century capitalism operated without regard for the long-term viability of their resource-base. Nature or the physical world was regarded as separate from the economy and available for its maximum transformation." (Urry, 2011: 117) Prior to now, the general consensus—among the advocates of capitalism as well as among its main critics—was (as Marx had it) that the underlying historical story associated with the rise of capitalism was one of the *humanization of nature*: the increasing capacity of people over time to transform natural products into commodities capable of improving the quality of their (human) lives, and an ever greater control by people collectively over the forces of nature (from famines to plagues) before which mankind in general had hitherto been powerless. The debate between capitalism and its critics was about the property laws and working conditions surrounding that transformation of the natural world, and about the distribution of the commodities so produced. It was not until recently about the adverse consequences of capitalist development on the condition of the natural world itself.

But it is now. The big question is whether we have already, or will soon, carry that process of humanization too far, in the process crossing some tipping point from which there will be no easy route of return, or no return at all. In a sense, that tipping point has long been recognized when attention has turned to military matters. The nuclear powers have had weapons capable of global destruction since the late 1940s; and certainly at the height of the Cold War (and particularly during the Cuban Missile Crisis of 1962) there was a general fear both in policy-making circles and among the populations of the Cold War combatants that the human race was looking over the abyss, and needed to pull back. How else are we to explain the willingness of so many governments since 1968 (currently 190 in total) to sign the Nuclear Non-Proliferation Treaty? But the question now is rather different: it is whether in economic terms we are approaching that same abyss. Is the development of modern industrially based, consumer-driven capitalist economies genera-ting such levels of pollution that it is fundamentally and permanently altering global temperatures, with potentially deva-stating effects on climate patterns and sea levels? Is that same development endangering the survival of the other species with which humans share the planet, both by destroying more and more of their natural habitats and by over-consuming the flesh and innards of those we eat? And are we as a species exhausting—by the level of our consumption—the basic raw materials on which we ultimately depend to reproduce and extend the modern economies on which our styles of life are currently so dependent?

Not everyone, of course, accepts the legitimacy of such questions, let alone the legitimacy of any of the answers to them presently on offer. Whether climate change is actually happening remains in dispute, at least in governing circles in the United States if less obviously elsewhere. (Coates, 2011: 92–9) Then not everyone accepts that, even if climate change is happening, there is anything unusual or man-made about that change. Climates, after all, have changed before. Not everyone accepts that, even if climate change is happening and is man-made, that the main driving force here derives from capitalism as a way of organiz-ing the economy, rather than simply from the industrially based nature of modern economies, however organized. After all, a major current polluter is China—now a larger polluter per head even than the European Union, the heartland of the original industrial revolution (Clarke, 2014)—and China is still officially a communist country. And not everyone who concedes that climate change and resource exhaustion is happening, and that both are man-made and driven by capitalist growth—not everyone accepting all those things buys the accompanying argument that we need therefore to abandon either capitalism or growth. (Butler & Holmes, 2007) There are plenty of people around convinced that, properly incentivized, capitalist economies are the best way of *stopping* the drift to environmental Armageddon—the best way, indeed, to actually reverse the trends.(Saunders, 1995: 69–76) There are even some convinced that green growth is the only viable growth strategy left available to fully developed capitalist economies.

So there is much to discuss and to think about when considering the relationship between capitalism and the environment. But certain things do seem fairly clear. The bulk of scientific opinion would appear to agree that the world is warming, and that the rate of warming is quickening because of increased global economic activity. (IPCC, 2014) There does seem to be a general recognition that air pollution is a real and growing problem, and that it affects the poor (within and between countries) more than it does the rich. (Boyce, 2014) There seems generalized agreement too that the natural habitat of many animals is heavily under challenge because of all this economic activity, and that in consequence the world does face, at the very least, a crisis of endangered species. (Naik, 2014) And there does seem to be a general recognition that enhanced global economic activity is putting very heavy pressure on the availability of vital resources, and that some of them at least—including some vital ones such as oil—are likely to run out within a recognizable and limited amount of time if current levels of their use are not somehow brought down and under control. (Urry, 2011: 76–82)

Where the current debate now turns, more than anywhere else, is on whether capitalism is best understood as being part of these widely recognized problems or best understood as being part of their solution; and that is where the whole notion of "the tragedy of the commons" comes into play. (Hardin, 1968) In the classic formulation of the problem, a commonly held piece of land was systematically over-grazed by the individuals who shared it, because no one had a personal short-term interest in the commons' long-term preservation. The normal solution was private ownership, the parceling up of the common land into private plots that each individual farmer had an interest in conserving long term. But the climate cannot be parceled off in such a fashion, or privately owned in bits. It is an unavoidably shared entity. It is the ultimate public good. So the logic of individual competition, rather than being the optimal solution to the tragedy of the environmental commons, threatens it directly. It is not in the interest of any individual/company to preserve the climate or defend the rain forests or slow down the rate of oil extraction. But it is in our collective interest that such restraint be shown. The question, therefore, is not whether, but how, to ensure that private interests do not block the full implementation of long-term collective needs: how, that is, to go green?

There is a body of literature out there insisting that the "how" involves nothing less than the entire deconstruction of capitalism itself. (Klein, 2014) It is a literature that often speaks of environmental degradation as: a "second contradiction of capitalism" (O'Connor, 1996), the basic class contradiction between capital and labor being the first. The American thinker James O'Connor understood this second contradiction as one "between capital accumulation and production conditions, driven by individual capitals seeking to shore up their profitability through cost-cutting which degrades, or fails to maintain, the material and social conditions of their production." (Spence, 2000: 85–6) He wrote of the warming of the atmosphere, acid rain, toxic waste and "the pesticide treadmill" (O'Connor, 1996: 207) as key examples of this contradiction deep in the heart of capitalism—a contradiction so entrenched that it cannot be managed away. This is the new Malthusianism: not global degradation through population growth per se, as the Reverend Malthus originally had it two centuries ago, but degradation resulting from the commodification of the natural environment, and from the inexorable pressure on finite natural resources created by the unrestrained consumption of increasingly affluent populations—their insatiable appetite for more and more man-made goods. It is the very productivity and avarice of capitalism that is said, in this literature, to be driving the global economy toward the precipice; such that only a brake on growth, a lowering of affluent living standards and a retreat from private ownership can (literally) stop the rot. (Coates, 2011: 108)

Perhaps fortunately, however, not everyone is so pessimistic. Herman Daly (1973), among others, has long proposed that what capitalism requires is the creation of a "steady state" economy in which "the state purposefully manages the 'material-energy throughput' of the economy at a level consistent with environmental sustainability, but the private sector remains the allocator of those economic resources made available to it by the democratic post-extractivist state." (Craig, 2014). There are accordingly plenty of plans afoot to harness conventional capitalist profit motives to the creation of green economic sectors, and to the slowing down of both climate change and resource depletion. (Coates, 2011: 109–13; Urry, 2011: 139–54) These invariably involve some mixture of progressively higher and tougher standards on the energy efficiency and environmental protection of existing technologies and products, the negotiation of international agreements on the lowering of greenhouse gas emissions as economies industrialize and grow, and the development of new carbon-free sources of power and transportation in old capitalisms and in new. Those initiatives and agreements are never easy to strike and are even harder to implement. Many large corporations stand to lose money and profits as energy sources shift, and many developing countries (China not least) object to being penalized for heavy industrial pollution now by governments whose economies, long ago, were themselves heavy polluters at a similar stage in their own development. But the Chinese government knows well enough that air quality of the kind now blanketing many Chinese cities in health-threatening smog cannot long go on; and in 2014 (when the UN held its latest bi-annual summit on climate control) 300,000 people clogged the streets of Manhattan alone, demanding stronger standards and tougher international enforcement. So environmental reform is definitely back on the political agenda. The trick now is to make that agenda real.

To environmental radicals, the term "green capitalism" may be an oxymoron, beyond our capacity to attain. They may be right, but probably it is better to think of green capitalism less as an impossibility than as a challenge—a challenge posing to all of us this critical question: can capitalism be managed into a new and successful growth period through its transformation from a high carbon-based production system to a low carbon-based one? Let us hope that ultimately it can; because if it cannot, the old adage of "don't drink the water and don't breathe the air" will become a debilitating reality for more and more of us, and our children and grandchildren will not thank us for the depleted legacy that we will have left behind for them to endure.

THE PROBLEM WITH CAPITALISM?

The scale of these problems—some directly anchored in basic capitalist processes and some deflected and refined by those processes though not directly caused by them—makes it at least legitimate to ponder whether our future would not be better if it were based on an entirely different system of economic organization. In each generation exposed to capitalism, some radical thinkers (and on occasions, whole labor movements) have come to that conclusion, and campaigned long and hard for some variety of a socialist alternative. But as yet to no avail. Any socialist alternative got a seriously bad press for as long as the Soviet Union was claiming to be one: for if socialism meant a centrally planned economy of gross inefficiency and a political system that was ostensibly democratic but actually tyrannical, who in his/her right mind would want anything to do with it? But that degenerated form of socialism is now fortunately gone and fading into memory, so there is real mileage to be had in thinking out again possible socialist scenarios (Nove, 1983; Breitenbach et al., 1990), if only to provide each of us with a benchmark against which to assess the predominant trajectories of capitalism itself. Whether we are moving toward a more socialist form of capitalism or toward a more libertarian form, and which is the more desirable form to pursue, are entirely legitimate questions to explore at this stage of global capitalist development. And with Freedom House still reporting in 2010 that "fully one third of the global population live in societies in which workers' rights suffer a significant degree of repression" (Freedom House, 2010), so too is the pursuit of forms of national accounting that measure economic success in terms of human well-being, and not just in terms of GDP. (NEF, 2009)

Yet the more realistic question in the modern age is not one of "capitalism or socialism." It is rather, "what form of capitalism" is best placed to deal with the problems we have just listed? If the movement you prefer is toward a more managed form of capitalism, then inevitably you will need to deal with free-rider issues connected with welfare provision, and with the disincentive effects of high levels of personal taxation. If, on the other hand, your direction of choice is toward a less regulated form of capitalism, then you will have to deal with issues associated with intensified inequalities of wealth and income, and with higher levels of insecurity for the vast majority of people denied access to that wealth. Most people facing that basic choice of direction— between an American kind of capitalism and a Western European kind of the sort mapped out in Chapter 2—tend to opt for a position somewhere in the middle, and you may do that too. But however you choose, the crucial point to note is that the kind of capitalism that will become prevalent in the next generation is something that, for the next generation, will itself be a matter of choice—their choice, so *your choice*. The future is in that sense constrained without being determined: the choice is limited, but the choice is still real.

The young Marx had a wonderful description of history as

nothing but the succession of the separate generations, each of which exploits the materials, the capital funds, the productive forces handed down to it by all preceding generations, and thus, on the one hand, continues the traditional activity in completely changed circumstances and, on the other, modifies the old circumstances with a completely changed activity.

The result, he wrote, was

a material result: a sum of productive forces, an historically created relation of individuals to nature and to one another, which is handed down to each generation from its predecessor; a mass of productive forces, capital funds and conditions which, on the one hand, is indeed modified by the new generation, but also on the other prescribes for it its conditions of life.

(Marx, 1843/1970: 57; 59)

We are at such a generational moment again. As the baby boomers leave the stage of history, it falls to their children and to their grandchildren to shape the world to a better standard than the one inherited from the past.

The task of a book such as this is to help you, as members of a rising generation, to clarify your chosen (and hopefully, better) direction of march. I can only hope that such a clarification is now well underway, and that your reading of this particular text has been of help in that endeavor.

GLOSSARY

Bourgeoisie: a French term with a long and complex history, but broadly equivalent to the English term "middle class." It is used in Marxist analysis as equivalent to the owners of capital (merchants, bankers, industrialists, even commercial farmers): men and women who employ the labor of others. The term is best contrasted to the term "proletariat," referring to those who do not own any capital and must therefore sell their labor power in return for wages—in English, the working class. It is also linked to the term "petty-bourgeoisie," used to describe those who own capital but do not employ labor (small shopkeepers, for example, who rely entirely on family members to run their store).

Capital: technically, capital is money invested in economic activity for the sole purpose of making more money. The term is, however, often also used to describe the forms in which the investment is held, as it moves from money through production and back to money: held as raw materials, as machinery and as unsold finished products. All are often labeled as a firm's capital. In general social analysis, the term is also sometimes used as a shorthand for the owners of capital—technically, the capitalists. Whenever you see the term "capital" used in analysis, therefore, you need to ask: does it mean investment funds, a firm's available resources or the people owning the business? Collectively, funds, resources and property owners constitute the economic and social phenomenon known as "capital."

Classical liberalism: the term liberalism has had a checkered career. Initially, as "classical liberalism," the term "liberalism" was used to refer to the ideas and writings of people favoring limited government and the extensive use of market mechanisms to allocate scarce resources, Later, as "new liberalism" it was used (and still is now, at least in the United States) to refer to exactly the reverse: to the ideas and writings of those keen to use government policies to improve the allocation of resources generated by market mechanisms alone. These days, those advocating the original "classical" package of policies (of limited government and only lightly regulated market outcomes) are normally labeled "neo-liberals" while those advocating strategic intervention into markets by public policy are normally labeled "social reformers," "social democrats," "liberals" or "progressives," depending on in which country they happen to be located.

Commodification: the provision and use of a good or service via the market mechanism of establishing a price which the recipient has to meet in order to consume the good or service in question.

Commodity: a good or service produced to be bought and sold.

Commodity chains: the new and complex production processes that involve components built in various parts of the global economy coming together in a product whose production is genuinely, therefore, international.

Conservatism: in the nineteenth century, in Western Europe at least, conservative thinkers were those challenging the rising liberal orthodoxy of limited government and free markets, often arguing for a degree of state paternalism on the basis of a recognition of human frailty and the limits of individual reason. As classical liberalism became the dominant thought pattern of the age, however, and public policy moved in its direction, conservatism's principles became something that its advocates wanted to conserve in the face of challenges from socialist/social democratic ideas and parties appealing directly to the working class; so that today conservative thought (and conservative politicians) are invariably defenders of limited government and free markets. See below, "neoliberalism." Not all conservatives today are neo-liberals, but certainly the gap between classical liberalism and modern conservatism has largely gone.

Coordinated market economies: the term used by Hall & Soskice (2001: 8) to capture common institutional characteristics of many Western European economies, where the linkages between firms, their employees, their suppliers and their financiers rely on long-term trust relationships more than on short-term, market-based ones.

Deindustrialization: that set of economic changes that reduces the contribution of the output of the manufacturing sector to total GDP, and the share of total employment provided by manufacturing industries. Normally a product of the shift of employment into service industries, deindustrialization occurs for both positive and negative reasons. Positive, when manufacturing employment shrinks because firms are so efficient they need fewer workers. Negative, when firms are so inefficient they lose market share and shed labor because they can no longer compete.

Enslaved: see "Slavery."

Fordism: the term developed by French Marxist sociologists from the 1970s to capture the complex character of modern economies: where production is based on semi-automated production systems of the kind first developed by Henry Ford, and where the viability of the firms requires both high productivity and output on the supply side and reliable and growing numbers of consumers on the demand side.

Free trade: the movement of goods and services across national boundaries without the imposition of tariffs, quotas or subsidies.

Friedman, Milton: (1912–2006) after Keynes, probably the most influential economist of the second half of the twentieth century, a powerful critic of Keynesian-inspired government policies and an advocate of monetarism, an adviser to Ronald Reagan and the recipient of the 1976 Nobel Prize for economics. He taught at the University of Chicago until his death in 2012.

Hayek, Friedrich: (1899–1992) along with Milton Friedman, an economist whose writings remain a major source of inspiration for those uneasy with government management of capitalist economies. His 1948 book *The Road to Serfdom* was and remains a major defense of individualism and classical liberalism.

Import substitution industrialization: that set of policies that protects new industries in a developing economy by blocking the entry of goods made by more established and efficient producers abroad. Widely used in both Asia and South America after 1945, ISI worked well if linked to penalties imposed by governments whenever local producers did not become more efficient. ISI worked less well if it simply protected local producers from pressures to modernize. In either case, ISI always needs replacing by more open trading arrangements after local industries have established themselves.

Keynesian economics: economic theory following the later writings of Keynes, seeing the flows of money in a modern economy as made up of consumption, investment, government spending and the difference between exports and imports, with government spending able to play a critical role in triggering greater flows (and therefore greater output and employment) when consumption has stalled and consequently private investment is hesitant.

Liberal market economies: the term developed by Hall and Soskice to capture common institutional characteristics of he US, UK and a number of other economies, where the linkages between firms, their employees, their suppliers and their financiers rely heavily on short-term, market-based calculations.

Liberalism: see above, "classical liberalism."

McCarthyism: the attack led by Senator Joe McCarthy between 1950 and 1956 on the supposed presence of communists in leading US institutions that triggered strong anti-left-wing feeling (and the dismissal/imprisonment of many people with progressive views) at the height of the early Cold War in the 1950s

Monetarism: the theory that there was a stable relationship between inflation and the money supply, which led conservative governments in the 1980s to cut public spending to bring prices under control.

Moral hazard: a moral hazard occurs whenever one party adopts a form of behavior which, if it generates adverse consequences, those consequences fall on another party. So, if I buy a house that I can't afford and then default on my payment, a moral hazard arises if my recklessness drags down the value of houses owned by people who only bought what they could afford. Likewise, if a mortgage broker deliberately sells me a mortgage he knows I can't afford but which earns him a fee, moral hazard issues arise. Needless to say, moral hazard was a big problem during the subprime mortgage crisis that triggered the 2008 financial collapse.

NAFTA: the North American Free Trade Agreement, signed between the governments of Mexico, Canada and the United States in 1994, slowly reducing tariff barriers between them in an attempt to stimulate the growth of industry and trade. Unlike the equivalent EU trade area, NAFTA did not permit the free movement of labor, nor did it see itself as a stage toward a single currency for the entire trade bloc.

Negative freedom: the distinction between negative and positive freedom was first popularized by Isaiah Berlin in the 1950s. Negative liberty is simply freedom from external constraints. You are free if no one stops you acting. Positive liberty requires more than a freedom from constraint. It also requires the possession of sufficient resources to fulfill your desires and potential. You are free if you have the capacity to act as you wish.

Neo-liberalism: the term used today to describe either people or policies prioritizing limited government regulation of private market forces or the overall system of light regulation and free trade called into existence under American international economic leadership since the presidency of Ronald Reagan.

New liberals: initially the term referred to that wing of the UK Liberal Party created by William Gladstone who first wanted to combine free trade and private enterprise with a degree of welfare support for the unemployed, old and destitute. That wing came to power in the United Kingdom in 1906, using their period of office to lay the foundations for the UK welfare state. The term "liberal" was later picked up and popularized—with that understanding of its meaning—by FDR and New Deal Democrats in the United States, who saw themselves similarly engaged, so creating a verbal confusion between "classical liberalism" and "new liberalism" that remains in place today. By the 1980s in the United Kingdom, Margaret Thatcher saw herself as a "liberal" (in the classical sense of limited government intervention in economic management) at the very moment when the term "liberal" in the United States meant opposing Thatcherite-like policies from the Reagan Administration!

OECD: the Organization for Economic Co-operation and Development—an international agency currently pulling together the leading thirty-four economies and liaising with at least a hundred more, charged with the development and advocacy of policies to improve the economic and social well-being of people around the globe.

Positive freedom: see above, "negative freedom."

Proletariat: a French term equivalent in meaning to the English term "working class." For more detail see above, "bourgeoisie."

Slavery: a form of production in which people are bought and sold, rather than as (in fully developed capitalisms) simply their labor power being bought and sold. In spite of the widespread abolition of slavery as a legitimate form of economic and social relationship, as late as 2014 there were still at least 35 million people locked in slavery worldwide. (Elliott, 2014) For the central importance of large-scale slavery to the rise of capitalism, see Blackburn (1997, 2011) and Beckert (2014).

Social democracy: a term used to describe the policies of moderate socialists in the post-1917 division of the global Left between those identifying with the Russian Revolution (so seeing their route to power as involving industrial struggles and eventually a military capture of the state, and calling themselves communists) and those preferring to use parliamentary institutions in established democracies as a slower but more peaceful electoral route to power. In modern parlance, with communism no longer a key player, social democracy refers to political parties (and their associated ideas) that favor the democratic management of a still predominantly privately owned economy and the development of extensive welfare services and worker rights.

Social wage: that part of your income that comes to you as a citizen rather than as a wage earner; so, for example, health care free at the point of use would be a part (actually a rather important part) of your social wage.

Weber, Max: (1864–1920) a leading German sociologist and thinker in the generation after Marx, and a major source for an alternative view to him of the origins, character and potential of capitalism.

WTO: the World Trade Organization, the only global international organization supervising world trade, via sets of trade agreements negotiated under its auspices and ratified by national parliaments. Established in 1995, it replaced the General Agreement on Tariffs and Trade established in 1948.

BIBLIOGRAPHY

All websites cited here were accessed on the day of publication, unless otherwise indicated.

Abendroth, Wolfgang (1974), *A Short History of the European Working Class*. London: New Left Books.

Achur, James (2011), *Trade Union Membership 2010*. London: Department for Business, Innovation & Skills.

Adams, Graham (1966), *The Age of Industrial Violence, 1910–15*. New York: Columbia University Press.

Adams, Richard (1997), "Value of £340 bn placed on housework last year," *The Guardian*, October 7.

Aglietta, Michel (1979), *A Theory of Capitalist Regulation*. London: New Left Books.

Albert, Michel (1993), *Capitalist Against Capitalism*. London: Whurr.

Arrighi, Giovanni (1991), "World Income Inequalities and the Future of Socialism," *New Left Review*, 189, pp. 39–65.

Arrighi, Giovanni (1994), *The Long Twentieth Century*. London: Verso.

Atzeni, Maurizio (Ed.) (2014), *Workers and Labour in a Globalised Capitalism*. London: Palgrave Macmillan.

Baumol, William J. (1994), "Multivariate Growth Patterns: contagion and common forces as possible sources of convergence," in William J. Baumol, Richard R. Nelson & Edward N. Wolff (Eds.), *Convergence of Productivity*. Oxford: Oxford University Press, pp. 62–85.

Beckert, Sven (2014), "Slavery and Capitalism," *The Chronicle of Higher Education: Review*, December 19, pp. B6–B9.

Beiler, Andreas, Lindberg, Ingemar & Pillay, Devan (Eds.) (2008), *Labour and the Challenges of Globalization*. London: Pluto Press.

Berg, Andrew & Ostry, Jonathan (2011), "Equality and Efficiency: Is there a trade-off between the two or do they do hand in hand?" *Finance & Development*, January, pp. 12–15.

Berger, Peter (1986), *The Capitalist Revolution*. New York: Basic Books.

Berger, Peter (1992), "The Uncertain Triumph of Democratic Capitalism," *Journal of Politics*, 3(3), July, pp. 7–16.

Blackburn, Robin (1997), *The Making of New World Slavery*. London: Verso.

Blackburn, Robin (2011), *The American Crucible*. London: Verso.

Bottomore, Tom (1985), *Theories of Modern Capitalism*. London: Allen & Unwin.

Bowles, Samuel, Edwards, Richard & Roosevelt, Frank (2005), *Understanding Capitalism*. New York: Oxford University Press.

Boyce, James (2014), *Shocking: New Research Shows Pollution Inequality in America Even Worse than Income Inequality*. Posted on Alternet, October 3, and available at www.alternet.org

Braudel, Fernand (1982), *Civilization and Capitalism 15th–18th Century: Volume II, The Wheels of Commerce*. London: William Collins, Sons.

Braudel, Fernand (1984), *Civilization and Capitalism 15th–18th Century: Volume III, The Perspective of the World*. London: William Collins, Sons.

Braverman, Harry (1974), *Labor and Monopoly Capitalism*. New York: Monthly Review Press.

Breitenbach, Hans, Burden, Tom & Coates, David (1990), *Features of a Viable Socialism*. New York: Harvester Wheatsheaf.

Brenner, Robert (1998), "The Economics of Global Turbulence," *New Left Review*, 229, pp. 1–265.

Briggs, Vernon M. (1996), *Mass Immigration and the National Interest*. Armonk, NY: M.E. Sharpe.

Butler, Stuart & Holmes, Kim (2007), *Twelve Principles to Guide US Energy Policy*. Washington DC: The Heritage Foundation.

Callaghan, James (1976), "Labour Party Conference Address," *Report of the 75th Annual Conference of the Labour Party*. London: The Labour Party.

Cassidy, John (2010), "What good is Wall Street?" *The New Yorker*, November 29.

Centeno, Miguel A. & Cohen, Joseph N. (2010), *Global Capitalism: A Sociological Perspective*. Cambridge: Polity.

Chandler, Alfred (1990), *Scale & Scope*. Boston, MA: Belknap Press.

Cingano, Frederico (2014), "Trends in Income Inequality and its Impact on Economic Growth," *OECD Social, Employment and Migration Working Papers*, No. 163. Paris: OECD Publishing.

Citizens Trade Campaign (2014), *CAFTA and the Scourge of Sweatshops*. Posted on Global Exchange and available at www.globalexchange.org/print/21206

Clarke, Pilita (2014), "China's emissions outstrip those of EU and US," *The Financial Times*, September 22.

CNN (2013), *World's Shortest Work Week*, July 10: available at http://money.cnn.com/gallery/news/economy/2013/07/10/worlds-shortest-work-weeks/8.html

Coates, David (1995), *Running the Country*. London: Hodder & Stoughton.

Coates, David (1999), "Models of Capitalism in the New World Order: the UK case," *Political Studies*, vol. 47(1), September, pp. 77–96.

Coates, David (2000), *Models of Capitalism: Growth and Stagnation in the Contemporary Era*. Cambridge: Polity.

Coates, David (2011), *Making the Progressive Case: Towards a Stronger US Economy*. New York: Continuum Books.

Coates, David (2015a), *America in the Shadow of Empires*. New York and London: Palgrave Macmillan.

Coates, David (2015b), "Varieties of Capitalism and 'the Great Moderation'," in Matthias Ebanau, Ian Bruff & Christian May (Eds.), *New Directions in Comparative Capitalisms Research*. London: Palgrave Macmillan, pp. 11–27.

Coates, David & Dickstein, Kara (2011), "A Tale of Two Cities: financial meltdown and the Atlantic divide," in Terrence Casey (Ed.), *The Legacy of the Crisis*. London: Palgrave Macmillan, pp. 60–78.

Craig, Martin (2014), "Locating Naomi Klein in the political economy of climate change," speri.comment, December 22: available at http://speri.dept.shef.ac.uk/2014/12/22/locating-naomi-klein-political-economy-climate-change/

Daly, Herman E. (1973), *Toward a Steady-State Economy*. San Francisco, CA: W.H. Freeman.

Daniels, Gary & McIlroy, John (Eds.) (2009), *Trade Unions in a Neo-Liberal World*. London: Routledge.

de Rothschild, Lady Lynn & Polman, Paul (2014), "The capitalism threat to capitalism," *Project Syndicate*, May: available at www.inclusivecapitalism.org/capitalist-threat-capitalism/

Devine, Fiona (1997), *Social Class in America and Britain*. Edinburgh: Edinburgh University Press.

Deyo, Frederic C. (1987), *The Political Economy of the New Asian Industrialism*. Ithaca, NY: Cornell University Press.

Diamond, Larry (2000), "The Global State of Democracy," *Current History*, December, pp. 412–18.

Dollar, David (2004), *Globalization, Poverty and Inequality since 1980*. World Bank Policy Research Working Paper No. 3333, June.

Donnan, Shawn, Bland, Ben & Burn-Murdoch, John (2014), "A slippery ladder: 2.8 billion people on the brink," *The Financial Times*, April 13: available at www.ft.com/intl/cms/s/2/e8f40868-c093–11e3-a74d-00144feabdc0.html#axzz3O4KjJ2W5

Dray, Philip (2010), *There is Power in a Union: The Epic Story of Labor in America*. New York: Doubleday.

Easterbrook, Gregg (2003), *The Progress Paradox*. New York: Random House.

Ebanau, Matthias, Bruff, Ian & May, Christian (Eds.) (2015), *New Directions in Comparative Capitalisms Research*. London: Palgrave Macmillan.

Economist, The (2014), "The tragedy of Argentina: a century of decline," *The Economist*, February 15: available at www.economist.com/news/briefing/21596582-one-hundred-years-ago-argentina-was-future-what-went-wrong-century-decline

Ehrenreich, Barbara (2007), "How we learned to stop having fun," *The Guardian*, April 7.

Elliott, Larry (2014), "Modern slavery affects more than 35 million people, report finds," *The Guardian*, November 17: available at www.theguardian.com/world/2014/nov/17/modern-slavery-35-million-people-walk-free-foundation-report

Esping-Andersen, Gósta (1990), *The Three Worlds of Welfare Capitalism*. Princeton, NJ: Princeton University Press.

Esping-Andersen, Gósta (Ed.) (2002), *Why We Need a New Welfare State*. Oxford: Oxford University Press.

Franko, Patrice (1999), *The Puzzle of Latin American Economic Development*. Lanham, MD: Rowman & Littlefield.

Freedom House (2010), *The Global State of Workers' Rights: Free Labor in a Hostile World*. Washington DC: Freedom House.

Freeman, Richard (2010), *What Really Ails Europe (and America): The Doubling of the Global Workforce*. Posted on The Globalist, March 5, available at www.theglobalist.com/what-really-ails-europe-and-america-the-doubling-of-the-global-workforce/

Frey, Bruno S. (2010), *Happiness: A Revolution in Economics*. Cambridge, MA: The MIT Press.

Frey, Bruno S. & Stutzer, Alois (2002), *Happiness and Economics*. Princeton, NJ: Princeton University Press.

Friedman, George (2010), "Germany and the Failure of Multiculturalism," *Geopolitical Weekly*, October 19: available at www.stratfor.com/weekly/20101018_germany_and_failure_multiculturalism

Friedman, Milton (1976), "The Line We Dare Not Cross," *Encounter*, November, pp. 11–14.

Friedman, Milton & Friedman, Rose (1980), *Free to Choose*. New York: Harcourt.

Friedman, Thomas (2006), "Empty pockets, angry minds," *The New York Times*, February 22.

Fukuyama, Francis (1992), *The End of History and the Last Man*. New York: The Free Press.

Fulcher, James (2004), *Capitalism: A Very Short Introduction*. Oxford: Oxford University Press.

Gallup (2014), *The "40-Hour" Workweek is Actually Longer—by Seven Hours*, August 29: available at www.gallup.com/poll/175286/hour-workweek-actually-longer-seven-hours.aspx?version=print

Gamble, Andrew (2014), *Crisis without End?* London: Palgrave Macmillan.

Gereffi, Gary (1990), "Paths of Industrialization: An Overview," in Gary Gereffi & D. Wyman (Eds.), *Manufacturing Miracles*. Princeton, NJ: Princeton University Press, pp. 3–31.

Giddens, Anthony (1971), *Capitalism and Modern Social Theory*. Cambridge: Cambridge University Press.

Goldblatt, David (1997), "Democracy in 'the Long Nineteenth Century': 1760–1919," in David Potter, David Goldblatt, Margaret Kiloh & Paul Lewis (Eds.), *Democratization*. Cambridge: Polity, pp. 46–70.

Gordon, David (1994), "Chickens Coming Home to Roost: from prosperity to stagnation in the postwar US economy," in M. Bernstein & D. Adler (Eds.), *Understanding American Economic Decline*. Cambridge: Cambridge University Press, pp. 34–76.

Gordon, Robert J. (2012), *Is U.S. Economic Growth Over? Faltering Innovation Confronts the Six Headwinds*. NBER Working Paper No. 18315: available at www.nber.org/papers/w18315 (accessed January 1, 2015).

Gordon, Robert J. (2014), *The Demise of U.S. Economic Growth: Restatement, Rebuttal and Reflections*. NBER Working Paper No. 19895: available at www.nber.org/papers/w19895 (accessed January 1, 2015).

Gunder Frank, Andre (1967), *The Development of Underdevelopment*. New York: Monthly Review Press.

Guttsman, W.L. (1981), *The German Social Democratic Party 1875–1933*. London: Allen & Unwin.

Haber, Stephen (Ed.) (1997), *How Latin America Fell Behind*. Stanford, CA: Stanford University Press.

Hall, Peter & Soskice, David (Eds.) (2001), *Varieties of Capitalism: The Institutional Foundations of Comparative Advantage*. Oxford: Oxford University Press.

Hardin, Garrett (1968), "The Tragedy of the Commons," *Science*, December, pp. 1243–68.

Harvey, David (1998), "The Geography of the Manifesto," in Leo Panitch & Colin Leys (Eds.), *The Communist Manifesto Now*. London: Merlin Press, pp. 49–74.

Harvey, David (2014), *Seventeen Contradictions and the End of Capitalism*. London: Profile Books.

Heymann, Jody & Earle, Alison (2010), *Raising the Global Floor*. Stanford, CA: Stanford University Press.

Hilton, Rodney (Ed.) (1976), *The Transition from Feudalism to Capitalism*. London: New Left Books.

Hodgson, Geoffrey (2014), "What is Capital? Economists and sociologists have changed its meaning: should it be changed back?" *Cambridge Journal of Economics*, 38, pp. 1063–86.

Huntington, Samuel P. (1996), "Democracy's Third Wave," in L. Diamond & M. Plattner (Eds.), *The Global Resurgence of Democracy*. Baltimore, MD: Johns Hopkins University Press, pp. 3–25.

Hutton, Will (1994), *The State We're In*. London: Cape, pp. 226–56.

Hutton, Will (2006), *The Writing on the Wall*. New York: Free Press.

Huws, Ursula (2014), *Labor in the Global Digital Economy*. New York: Monthly Review Press.

ILO (2014), *World of Work Report*. Geneva: International Labor Organization.

Infoplease (2014), *Life Expectancy at Birth by Race & Sex, 1930–2010*: available at www.infoplease.com/ipa/A0005148.html (accessed January 1, 2015).

IPCC (2014), *Climate Change 2014: Impacts, Adaptions, and Vulnerability*. Report published March 31: available at www.who.int/globalchange/environment/climatechange-2014-report/en/

Jessop, Bob (1990), *State Theory: Putting the Capitalist State in its Place*. Cambridge: Polity Press.

Kay, John (2003), *The Truth About Markets*. London: Allen Lane.

Kendall, Walter (1969), *The Revolutionary Movement in Britain 1900–21*. London: Weidenfeld & Nicholson.

Keynes, John Maynard (1936), *The General Theory of Employment, Interest and Money*. London: Macmillan.

Kidron, Michael (1967), *The Permanent Arms Economy*. Harmondsworth: Penguin.

Klein, Naomi (2014), *This Changes Everything: Capitalism vs the Climate*. New York: Simon & Schuster.

Kotz, David M., McDonough, Terrence & Reich, Michael (Eds.) (1994), *Social Structures of Accumulation: The Political Economy of Growth & Crisis*. Cambridge: Cambridge University Press.

Kuhn, Thomas (1962), *The Structure of Scientific Revolutions*. Chicago, IL: The University of Chicago Press.

La Barca, Guiseppe (2013), *International Trade in the 1970s*. London: Bloomsbury.

Lakner, Christoph & Milanovic, Branko (2014), *Global Income Distribution: From the Fall of the Berlin Wall to the Great Recession*. World Bank Policy Research Paper No. 6719: available at http://papers.ssrn.com/sol3/papers.cfm?abstract_id=2366598

Layard, Richard (2005), *Happiness: Lessons from a New Science*. London: Penguin.

Lazonick, William (1991), *Business Organization and the Myth of the Market Economy*. Cambridge: Cambridge University Press.

Lee, David & Turner, Bryan (Eds.) (1996), *Conflicts about Class*. London: Longman.

Lippit, Victor D. (2005), *Capitalism*. London: Routledge.

Little, Ben (2014), "A Growing Discontent: class and generation under neo-liberalism," *Soundings* No. 56, Spring, pp. 27–40.

Logie, Phyllis (2013), "The History of the Arawak People," *Ancient History*, October, pp. 4–7.

McCormick, Michael (2001), *Origins of the European Economy: Communications and Commerce 600–900*. Cambridge: Cambridge University Press.

McNally, Christopher A. (2007), "China's Capitalist Transition: the making of a new variety of capitalism," in Lars Mjóset & Tommy H. Clausen (Eds.), *Capitalisms Compared*. Amsterdam: Elsevier, pp. 177–203.

Maddison, Angus (1995), *Explaining the Economic Performance of Nations*. Aldershot: Edward Elgar.

Marx, Karl (1843), *The German Ideology*. London: Lawrence & Wishart, 1970.

Marx, Karl (1857), "Preface to a Contribution to the Critique of Political Economy," in Karl Marx & Frederick Engels, *Selected Works*. London: Lawrence & Wishart, 1968, pp. 181–5.

Marx, Karl (1867), *Capital: Volume 1*. London: J.M. Dent & Sons, 1930.

Marx, Karl & Engels, Frederick (1848), "The Communist Manifesto," in Karl Marx & Frederick Engels, *Selected Works*. London: Lawrence & Wishart, 1968, pp. 31–63.

Meltzer, Allan H. (2012), *Why Capitalism?* Oxford: Oxford University Press.

Mielants, Eric H. (2007), *The Origins of Capitalism and the Rise of the West*. Boston, MA: Temple University Press.

Mishel, Lawrence, Bernstein, Jared & Shierholz, Heidi (2009), *The State of Working America*. Ithaca: Cornell University Press.

Mitchell, David (1970), *1919: Red Mirage*. London: Cape.

Naik, Gautam (2014), "Study: half of wildlife lost in 40 years," *The Wall Street Journal*, October 1.

NEF (2009), *National Accounts of Well-Being*. London: New Economics Foundation.

Nettl, Peter (1966), *Rosa Luxemburg*. Oxford: Oxford University Press (2 volumes).

Nove, Alex (1983), *The Economics of Feasible Socialism*. London: Allen & Unwin.

O'Connor, James (1996), "The Second Contradiction of Capitalism," in Tim Benton (Ed.), *The Greening of Marxism*. New York: Guildford Press, pp. 197–221.

Okun, Arthur Melvin (1975), *Equality and Efficiency: The Big Trade-Off*. Washington DC: Brookings Institution Press.

Otteson, James R. (2011), *Adam Smith*. New York: Bloomsbury.

Page, John (2014), *Africa's Failure to Industrialize: Bad Luck or Bad Policy?* Washington DC: Brookings, November 14: available at www.brookings.edu/blogs/africa-in-focus/posts/2014/11/19-africa-failure-industrialize-page

Perelman, Michael (2011), *The Invisible Handcuffs of Capitalism*. New York: Monthly Review Press.

Pierson, Paul (Ed.) (2001), *The New Politics of the Welfare State*. Oxford: Oxford University Press.

Piketty, Thomas (2014), *Capital in the Twenty-First Century*. Cambridge, MA: Belknap Press.

Pinheiro, Armanda, Gill, Indermit, Servan, Luis & Thomas, Mark Roland (2004), *Brazilian Economic Growth 1900–2000: Lessons and Policy Implications*. Washington DC: Inter-American Development Bank.

Piovani, Chiara & Li, Minqi (2011), "One Hundred Million Jobs for the Chinese Workers: why China's current model of development is unsustainable," *Review of Radical Political Economy*, 43(1), pp. 77–94.

Plender, John (2012), "Capitalism in crisis: the code that forms a bar to harmony," *The Financial Times*, January 8.

Porter, Michael (2014), *Social Progress Index 2014*: available at www.hbs.edu/faculty/Pages/item.aspx?num=47348 (accessed January 1, 2015).

Rampel, Catherine (2010), "South Koreans put in most hours," *The New York Times*, May 12.

Rostow, W.W. (1960), *The Stages of Economic Growth*. Cambridge: Cambridge University Press.

Sandel, Michael J. (2012), *What Money Can't Buy: The Moral Limits of Markets*. New York: Penguin.

Sassoon, Donald (1996), *One Hundred Years of Socialism*. New York: The Free Press.

Satz, Debra (2012), *Why Some Things Should Not Be for Sale: The Moral Limits of Markets*. New York: Oxford University Press.

Saunders, Peter (1995), *Capitalism: A Social Audit*. Buckingham: Open University Press.

Segal, Paul (2014), "The Problem of Riches," *Renewal*, Vol. 22, July, pp. 134–42.

Selwyn, Benjamin (2014), "Twenty-First-Century International Political Economy: a class-relational perspective," *European Journal of International Relations*, December, pp. 1–25.

Shell, Ellen Ruppel (2009), *Cheap: The High Cost of Discount Culture*. New York: The Penguin Press.

Short, Kevin (2014), *The Worst Places on the Planet to Be a Worker*. Posted on The Huffington Post, May 28, and available at www.huffingtonpost.com/2014/05/28/worst-countries-workers_n_5389679.html

Skidelsky, Robert & Skidelsky, Edward (Eds.) (2013), *Are Markets Moral?* London: Centre for Global Studies.

Smith, Adam (1776), *The Wealth of Nations*. London: Ward Lock, 1812.

Solow, Robert (2008), "The German Story," in Gerhard Bosch & Claudia Weinkopf (Eds.), *Low-Wage Work in Germany*. New York: Russell Sage Foundation, pp. 1–14.

Spence, Martin (2000), "Capital against Nature: James O'Connor's theory of the second contradiction of capitalism," *Capitalism & Class*, 72, pp. 81–109.

Spriggs, William E. & Price, Lee (2005), *Productivity Growth and Social Security's Future*. Washington DC: EPI Issue Brief #208, May 11.

Stiglitz, Joseph (2008) *Report by the Stiglitz Commission on the Measurement of Economic Performance and Social Progress*. Paris: available at www.stiglitz-sen-fitoussi.fr/en/index.htm (accessed January 1, 2015).

Streeck, Wolfgang (1997), "Can the German Model Survive?" in Colin Crouch & Wolfgang Streeck (Eds.), *Political Economy of Modern Capitalism*. London: Sage, pp. 33–54.

Streeck, Wolfgang (2014), "How Will Capitalism End?" *New Left Review*, 87, May–June, pp. 35–64.

Summers, Lawrence (2013), "Why stagnation may prove to be the new normal," *The Financial Times*, December 15.

Summers, Lawrence (2014), "Washington must not settle for secular stagnation," *The Financial Times*, January 5.

Taylor, Robert (1993), *The Trade Union Question in British Politics*. Oxford: Blackwell.

Therborn, Goran (1977), "The Rule of Capital and the Rise of Democracy," *New Left Review*, 103, pp. 3–41.

Thompson, E.P. (1963), *The Making of the English Working Class*. London: Gollancz.

Tomkins, Richard (2003), "How to be happy," *Financial Times*, March 8–9.

UNDP (2013), *Humanity Divided: Confronting Inequality in Developing Countries*. Report published January 28.

Urry, John (2011), *Climate Change and Society*. Cambridge: Polity.

van Ark, Bart & Timmer, Marcel P. (2002), "Realising Growth Potential: South Korea and Taiwan, 1960 to 1998," in Angus Maddison (Ed.), *The Asian Economies in the Twentieth Century*. Cheltenham: Edward Elgar, pp. 226–244.

Walby, Sylvia (1991), *Theorizing Patriarchy*. Oxford: Blackwell.

Wallerstein, Immanuel (1983), *Historical Capitalism*. London: Verso.

Wickham, Chris (2005), *Framing the Early Middle Ages: Europe and the Mediterranean 400–800*. Oxford: Oxford University Press.

Wilkinson, Richard & Pickett, Kate (2009), *The Spirit Level*. London: Allen Lane.

Williams, Raymond (1976), "Capitalism," in Raymond Williams, *Keywords: A Vocabulary of Culture and Society*. New York: Oxford University Press, pp. 142–4.

Wills, Gabrielle (2009), *South Africa's Informal Economy: Statistical Profile*. Cambridge, MA: WIEGO Working Paper, April.

Wolf, Martin (2003), "Humanity on the move: the myths and realities of international migration," *The Financial Times*, July 30.

Wolf, Martin (2014), "Why inequality is such a drag on economies," *The Financial Times*, September 30.

Wolff, Richard D. & Renick, Stephen A. (2012), *Contending Economic Theories: Neoclassical, Keynesian and Marxian*. Cambridge, MA: MIT Press.

World Bank (2014), *Employment in Industry (%age of Total Employment)*: available at http://data.worldbank.org/indicator/SL.IND.EMPL.ZS (accessed January 1, 2015).

Zaretsky, Eli (1986), *Capitalism, the Family, and Personal Life*. New York: Perennial Library.

INDEX

accumulation crises 101
acid rain 163
active labor market policy 37
administrative guidance 30
affluence 17, 40, 111, 113
Afghanistan 158
Africa 4, 115, 145, 156, 158
agricultural day laborers 9, 10, 57
agriculture 13, 27, 54
Albert, Michel 26
Arawak people 2
Argentina 21, 77, 115
aristocracies 5, 7, 8, 53,118
aristocracy of labor 60, 61
Armenian genocide 156
Arrighi, Giovanni 114
arsenal of democracy, 31
artisans 9, 54
Asian Tiger economies 46
Australia 26, 35, 133
Austria 26

baby boomers 43, 70, 116, 127, 144,
    147, 167
balance of class forces 6, 69, 71, 76,
    102–3
Bangladesh 78

banks 2, 3, 9, 30
Baumol, W.J. 113
Berger, Peter 128, 133, 134
Bin Laden, Osama 158, 159
Black Death 7
Bolsheviks 14, 64
bourgeoisie 53, 65, 90, 168
Brazil 21, 48, 77, 78, 114, 115, 121
BRIC (Brazil, Russia, India and China)
    economies 24, 48, 115
British Empire 155
Bush, George W. 99

Callaghan, James 98
Canadian economy 26, 35
capital 16, 168; controls on 45; export
    of 48; flight of 74
capital-capital accord 15
capital-labor accord 15, 18
capitalism, crises 19, 92, 101; definition
    of xv–xvi, 4, 21–2; dynamics 19;
    golden age of 68, 70, 72; history of
    xiv, 8–11, 56; instability and 19;
    theories of xiv; types of xvi, 15;
    ubiquity of 1–4; varieties of xvi, 9,
    15, 28–46
capitalist class 6, 7, 8